DATE DUE

Demco, Inc. 38-293

NOV '90

Women Who Shop
Too Much

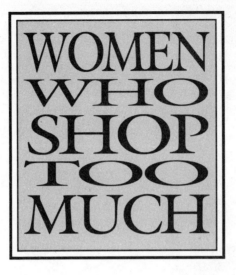

WOMEN WHO SHOP TOO MUCH

Overcoming the Urge to Splurge

Carolyn Wesson

St. Martin's Press/New York

Design by Amelia R. Mayone

The quote from Anne Morrow Lindbergh's *Locked Rooms and Empty Doors* is here
reprinted by permission of Harcourt, Brace Jovanovich, Inc. Copyright © 1974 by
Anne Morrow Lindbergh.

A Life Stress Scale is here reprinted by permission from Thomas H. Holmes and
Richard H. Rache, from "The Social Readjustment: Rating Scale," *Journal of Psychosomatic Research* 11 (1967):213–18.

Women's Life Events Scale and the Fast-Pace Profile for Women are here reprinted by
permission from Villiard Books, a division of Random House, from *Quick Fixes and
Small Comforts* by Georgia Witkin. Copyright © 1988 by Georgia Witkin-Lanoie.

Are You a Drama Seeker? reprinted by permission of Jeremy Tarcher, Inc., Los
Angeles. Copyright © 1988 by Joy Davidson, from *The Agony of It All.*

"Common Problems in Co-Addicted Relationships" is here reprinted by permission
from Health Communications, Inc., from *In Sickness and in Health* by Mary Stuart.
Copyright © 1988.

Excerpt from *Struggle for Intimacy* by Janet Woititz is here reprinted by permission
from Health Communications, Inc. Copyright © 1985.

Library of Congress Cataloging-in-Publication Data

Wesson, Carolyn.
        Women who shop too much : overcoming the urge to splurge / Carolyn
Wesson.
        p. cm.
        ISBN 0-312-03957-3
        1. Compulsive shopping.   2. Women—Mental health.   I. Title.
    RC569.5.S56W47   1990
    616.85'227—dc20   89-24117

First Edition

10 9 8 7 6 5 4 3 2 1

To my loving parents
Lorraine and George Hayes

Contents

Dramatis Personae

(Cast of Characters)

The following are brief profiles of the women and men who appear in this book. Many people chose their own fictional names, but the stories are genuine.

ANDREA. A confirmed bargain hunter who becomes hooked on the "Home Shopping Network."

ASHLEY. Age twenty-nine, she feels she has to have the best in everything she buys, despite the fact that she's already had to file bankruptcy once.

BETH. Goes on shopping sprees but rarely wears what she buys.

DEENA. A crafts fair junkie who shops every weekend to avoid her unhappy marriage.

DINELLE. Is happy shopping in boutiques but feels like crying when she goes into a department store.

DON. Jessica's workaholic husband.

EVE. Periodically tries to curb her excessive charging by freezing her credit cards, then microwaves them back to life when she's ready for another spree.

GWYNETHE. Overcomes her lifelong shopping addiction when she gets a job that utilizes her creativity.

IRIS. Her husband has blown two million dollars since his retirement two years ago.

JENNIFER. Abused as a child, she now uses her beauty, perfectionism, and clothes to hide her numerous insecurities.

JESSICA. Lives on a remote island off the East Coast but still manages to shop six hours a day.

JULIE. Grew up on the "wrong side of the tracks" but now owns a boutique and spends thirty thousand dollars a year on her wardrobe.

MARILYN. Her low self-esteem leads her into destructive relationships and addictive spending, until she finds an exciting substitute.

PAT. A multimillionaire who hides purchases from her husband and doesn't understand why.

ROSA. Feels powerless to change many things in her life, so she shops to forget her troubles and to feel in control.

VICKI. Enters therapy for her spending addiction when her husband discovers she has run up twenty-five thousand dollars in credit card charges. Her successful therapy is followed throughout the book.

Acknowledgments

To my husband, Gil: How do I say thank you for living through my splurges, for supporting me through the two years it took to get this book to press, for helping me understand this baffling computer, and for spending dozens of hours editing and formatting every page to your exacting standards. My right brain honors your left, my heart says, "We've done it, let's go play!"

To my agent, Laurie Harper: Thank you for believing, and believing, and believing. What a joy to have you in my corner.

To my editor, Bob Weil, and his assistant, Jon Gertner: My deepest gratitude for your splendid editing and for the condensed course you gave me in writing and grammar.

To Susan Einstein Schwartz: Thanks to the woman who thought up the subtitle for this book in about twenty minutes and generously gave it to me to use.

To the very special women who graciously agreed to be interviewed for this book, thank you. You were extraordinarily open about your feelings and lives, and the information you shared was invaluable. A special thanks to Vicki, for opening the door to a very private part of her life—her therapy sessions.

Introduction

At different times in my life, shopping has been a salve to soothe my unhappy feelings. When I was mad at my husband, I'd zoom downtown for a little revenge raid. My friends frequently handled their feelings in the same way, and we'd chuckle about our similarities. Then several distressing events in my life converged over a three-year period, and my shopping escalated to a two-year spree. When Imelda Marcos's prodigious spending became public knowledge, it dawned on me that it wasn't just Jackie Onassis, my friends, and I who were out shopping; *it was a global problem*. Relieved and intrigued, I began the research for this book.

My first step was to read as much as I could about shopping addiction, but in 1987 there wasn't much being written. Excessive shopping was still kind of a joke, like football widows who had to resort to Astroturf nighties to get attention from their sports-addicted husbands. Slowly, though, the picture began to change. Articles appeared in women's magazines about shopaholics, and Phil and Oprah interviewed them on their shows. But most women with the problem were reluctant to talk about it. They were embarrassed and ashamed. Consequently, I started my interviewing with my friends and acquaintances. They, in turn, would say, "Oh, you've got to talk to 'so and so.' She's really got it bad." So and so would then introduce me to another friend, and that process was the basis of the interviews that appear in this book. Unfortunately, I didn't get to interview as many people from different socioeconomic and ethnic groups as I would have wished.

I live in one of the wealthiest counties in the world—Santa Clara County (in northern California), also known as Silicon Valley. So there are many bright, wealthy, stressed, and anxious people living here—people who are ripe for addiction.*

This, in turn, raises the issue of men. Don't some of them shop and spend excessively? The answer, of course, is yes. But I focused on women for two reasons. First, women traditionally have been society's shoppers, and that hasn't changed a great deal. Second, I believe that most men have different addictions: alcohol, drugs, and process addictions such as work, television, sports, and projects. For this reason I chose to limit the book to women. By doing so, I'm not implying that men don't have shopping or spending problems; I just think they express their unhappiness in other ways.

Are all women who shop a lot troubled? No. I've met some very well adjusted women who simply get a kick out of shopping. Yet I think even these women will benefit from reading *Women Who Shop Too Much*, because it invites the reader to assess just how satisfying shopping and spending really are.

That brings us full circle to the message of this book. Balanced shopping and spending are delicious parts of life; they are not something we'd want to give up entirely. But we live in a highly acquisitive society that has taught us to believe that possessions bring happiness. I've come to question that. Through my own battle with shopping and spending I found a slew of other activities that have brought me far *greater* pleasure. Things that nourish my soul. Sweet William, for one. He's the guy standing next to me inside the back cover.

It is my hope that reading *Women Who Shop Too Much* will help you find more excitement and joy in your life, as well.

---

*According to Warren Chaumont, former director of Marketing for Valley Fair, one of the area's largest shopping malls, "The buying power in Santa Clara County is equivalent to the total buying income of eighteen states combined."

Friday, February 24, 1933

I am doing it right over again. I am sick of clothes and gewgaws and bags and advertisements and newspaper clippings and society pages and the new *Vogue* and fittings and the main floor of department stores and the radio-jazz and magazines and hairdressers. I am sick sick to death of them. But I clutch at them madly, like smoking or drinking—anything to keep from thinking.

—Anne Morrow Lindbergh,
Locked Rooms and Empty Doors

Part One

The Reasons

Chapter 1

Women Who Shop
Too Much

When prospective buyers toured the Turner's home, they invariably came to a dead stop in front of Sandi's immense walk-in closet. Astonished, they gazed at dozens of pairs of shoes neatly lined around the perimeter of the closet floor. Her dresses, evening gowns and furs, and pants outfits hung above them in color groups that coordinated with matching purses on the shelf above. Most prospective buyers just gaped at Sandi's clothes, shook their heads, and continued to tour the rest of the house. But one afternoon a man who was previewing homes for his family in Illinois took one look at Sandi's closet and flatly refused to see the rest of the house. Perplexed, his real estate agent trailed him down two flights of stairs, out the front door, and asked what was wrong. Glowering, the man replied, "There's no way I'm *ever* going to let my wife see that *one woman* owns that many clothes."

Sandi thought the incident was funny. She was used to other people's shocked reactions to her vast wardrobe and they didn't bother her a whit. She has always loved clothes,

3

and ever since high school she's taken most of her wages and "put them on her back." She equally enjoys buying her husband handsome clothes, and they both relish looking terrific. Wryly, they refer to their clothes as their "Ken and Barbie outfits." Is Sandi a shopaholic or an addicted shopper? Neither. She is what I call a recreational shopper.

THREE KINDS OF SHOPPERS

Gathered at one end of the shopping continuum are women like Sandi, who just love to shop. Their shopping doesn't fill any particular deep-seated psychological need. They are like avid sports fans. They enjoy the whole experience, but that's it. Their feelings don't run much deeper, although they may still spend vast amounts of money. They are recreational shoppers. Danger begins toward the middle and opposite end of the continuum, where we find shopaholics and addicted shoppers. As you read this book about women who love to shop, you will gradually understand the differences. See if you recognize any of the following symptoms.

SHOPAHOLICS

Shopaholics, a group of millions of women who occupy the middle of the shopping spectrum, are passionate about shopping in the same way that chocoholics love chocolate. They can go without chocolate for just so long, and then they've got to have some. It's the same way with shopaholics. *Occasionally* they also will use shopping to satisfy both conscious and unconscious feelings. Hours in the mall will perk up a boring, empty day; a new dress can boost sagging self-esteem, while a Gucci bag snaps with revenge. Sometimes a shopaholic may buy herself something new and stupendous to celebrate an achievement. Either way, shopping is a temporary pick-me-up that leaves the shopper feeling *better* afterward.

The words *occasionally* and *better* are italicized because they are key factors in determining what kind of shopper you are. That's because shopping, like other quick fixes, isn't destructive as long as it isn't overused. It's not overused as a way of avoiding problems, nor is it abused to the point where you feel worse, not better. Throughout the book you will find portraits or mini–case studies of women with varying degrees of shopping problems. Here is the first vignette, a description of a woman I call Pat, who exhibits many of the symptoms of the shopaholic.

Portrait of a Shopaholic

Pat nudges back her menagerie of yappy, pint-sized dogs and quickly slips out the front door of her two million–dollar home overlooking Silicon Valley. Jumping into her little silver Mercedes, she winds down her long, snaking driveway and heads for the highway. A right turn will take her to the boutique-dotted streets of Saratoga. A left leads to the huge discount hardware store and K Mart. She turns left.

Pulling into K Mart's parking lot, she notices that her heart is racing. She parks, checks her reflection in the rearview mirror and chuckles. Sure enough, she's so excited that her face is flushed; this happens every time she goes shopping. Carefully she locks her car and sprints across the parking lot. The automatic doors whoosh open and Pat plunges inside for two hours of concentrated shopping.

As she pushes her cart up and down the crowded aisles, she's bombarded by feelings. She's excited by the challenge of trying to find a bargain. That's why she is in K Mart—the store's loaded with them. Ironically, even though she's keyed up, Pat also begins to unwind and relax. She blanks out the world when she's in a store; there's just her and the merchandise.

Pat has several inflexible rules about her favorite pastime. She has to go up and down every aisle; if she doesn't, she might miss a bargain. She also has to buy something; it kills her to leave a store emptyhanded.

Relaxed and delighted with her purchases, Pat leaves K Mart with two bags of goodies. One bag is full of things for the house—silk flowers, a towel, bath salts, and a knickknack that struck her fancy. The other bag contains a pair of thongs, a dress, and a shirt and pants outfit. Pat could easily afford to buy all of her clothes in Paris, but she claims that wouldn't be any fun. She gets a much bigger kick out of buying a snappy-looking outfit from K Mart, and then pretending she's forgotten where she purchased it when asked by an admiring friend. "I like to think of myself as clever," she says. "It's a game of wits." Her little game of deceit is played out in her marriage as well. Driving home, she reviews what she's bought and decides which things she'll show her husband Bob and which things she'll hide.

It's not that Bob would criticize. He wouldn't. Rather, Pat relishes the feeling of getting away with something—of pulling off a scam. Even though she only occasionally hides things, she is concerned about what it means. Her unease is appropriate—not because she's doing anything awful; she isn't. But because something unconscious, hidden from her awareness, is controlling her behavior. That suggests she has feelings or needs that aren't being addressed, either by herself or in her relationships.

Pat began hiding things during her first marriage. Her husband was tight with money, and even though Pat worked, her husband insisted on being consulted about any purchases over five dollars. He rarely approved. Unable to budge him from his unreasonable and authoritarian position, Pat went underground. She bought things and then hid them until she felt it was safe to bring them out. If her husband asked if she had a new dress on, for instance, she would deny it and duck behind that age-old feminine subterfuge, "No, I've had this for ages." Given her relationship with that husband, such duplicity makes perfect sense. But her first marriage ended twenty years ago. Why is she still doing it? Habit? That might have explained her behavior in the beginning of her second marriage, when she wasn't sure how her new husband would react to her spending. But Bob is generous, so her behavior appears illogical. More fertile clues lie in Pat's personality and her current marriage.

Like many other shopaholics, Pat's personality is a paradox. Her extroverted, outspoken, fun-loving, friendly exterior masks a tense, perfectionistic, ambitious, and nonassertive interior. Thus, her shopping ploys actually may be a form of rebellion by a rather driven, perhaps passively aggressive, woman. She also may be trying to pull one over on her brilliant husband, who often bests her with his impeccable and infuriating logic. Her hidden purchases represent a kind of power. "I may not be able to defeat you directly, in conversations and in arguments, but I can experience a sense of strength and equality through my secret purchases tucked away on the closet shelf," she is saying. Although Pat's two husbands differ in their attitudes about spending and shopping, both men are dominating, powerful, and parental. Unable, at times, to fight and win on the open battlefield, she unconsciously uses the same mechanism—hiding things—to even the score. If this was Pat's only way of fighting things out with Bob, then she would be a likely candidate for addiction. Fortunately, it's just one weapon in her arsenal. More often she hashes things out directly.

In her current position Pat is much better off than an addicted shopper, but like all addictions, the slide from use to abuse is slow, subtle, and accompanied by the big D—denial. Consequently, recognizing when a shopper has crossed the line from shopaholic to addicted usually isn't noticeable. However, there are warning signs. The first is frequency. If you're spending more and more time or money shopping, without a clearcut purpose or need, you're headed for trouble. Or, if you're beginning to think about it obsessively, that can spell trouble as well. The second warning sign is feeling guilty and ashamed after spending or shopping. I'll explain more about that in the next section. Feeling anxious while you're shopping is another symptom that your shopping is getting out of hand. That vague, worried feeling is your conscience at work, saying, "Beware! This isn't good for you."

ADDICTED SHOPPERS/SPENDERS

Addicted shoppers and addicted spenders are terms that can be used almost interchangeably. They describe people addicted to the same process. It's just that addicted shoppers get their high out of shopping and addicted spenders get theirs out of spending money. To simplify things, addicted spenders and shoppers will be lumped together into one category here—addicted shoppers. At any given time there are, conservatively, about five million addicted shoppers combing the malls, jetting to Europe, or driving sexy cars. Most are in debt, but some aren't. What they have in common is obsessive thinking and compulsive behavior, which are used to escape problems, relieve anxiety, and feel alive.

They are also trying to avoid painful feelings, which they do by keeping their charge cards zipping through those little oblong machines. At first it works. They feel wonderful, carefree, and excited when they shop or spend. But then it takes more and more spending to get the same feeling. In the beginning a pretty little polyester blouse gets spirits soaring. Now it takes a whole rainbow of silky blouses to get the same rush.

As the addiction progresses, compulsive shoppers feel driven to shop daily, or even hourly. If they aren't shopping, they're thinking about it and planning their next hit. Shopping takes over lives in much the same way that drinking dominates the life of an alcoholic. They shop simply to shop. In fact, they may not wear or use most of what they buy—tags dangle from unworn dresses, eight cigarette lighters from Cartier go unused, sheets stay wrapped in their tight little cases—because addicted shoppers lose interest in their purchases once they get them home. The high comes from the process of shopping, not from the items they buy. They used to feel grand after spending; now they feel bleak, guilty, depressed, and ashamed because they've been "bad" (by shopping). And it is just this cyclical process of highs followed by lows that signals addiction. Such shoppers proceed to spend more in order to feel better, which only makes them feel worse. Their self-control disappears, their self-esteem plummets, and their bill basket overflows. To underscore the differences between shopaholics and addicted spenders, shopaholics only *occasionally* use shopping to alter their mood, and they generally feel *better* after shopping. Addicted shoppers, on the other hand,

1. *Routinely* shop and spend to avoid or to fix feelings;

2. Begin their shopping expeditions with heart-palpitating highs, but find they end in regret, self-recrimination, and depression;

3. Increase the frequency of their spending without reason;

4. May incur substantial debt;

5. Often never use their purchases.

How addicted shoppers get into such a pickle varies from person to person, but the underlying causes are twofold: they have found a way to feel better about themselves, and, at the same time, they have discovered a sure-fire way to banish unwanted thoughts, feelings, and problems. Some of the feelings they want to escape are: emptiness, depression, anxiety, anger, powerlessness, and rejection.

Ashley's spiral into addicted spending seemed to begin with a perfectly legitimate purpose—opening a store of her own. However, owning her own store, coupled with her unconscious wish to please her critical and rejecting father, eventually led to bankruptcy. Ashley was forced to build a new life from the ashes left behind by her shopping addiction. Let's take a look.

An Addicted Shopper

Radiating that kind of wholesome, fresh-scrubbed look of young women who pose for Cover Girl makeup ads, Ashley has long, honey-colored hair tucked behind her ears, beautiful wide-spaced blue eyes, terrific bone structure. Tall, she looks like a model and in fact would like to be one, but she realizes that she's almost too old at twenty-nine. Modeling is just one of her dreams. She'd also like to own a boutique specializing in unique and elegant lingerie.

It's this latter goal, owning a boutique, that got her into trouble. At least it was mostly that. The other factor is her obsession with having the best of everything: apartments, clothes, sun glasses, food, bikes. It doesn't matter what it is; she wants the top of the line or she doesn't want it at all. Emphasizing her point, she nodded toward her Gucci bag sitting on the floor, saying, "Now I have to have a Louis Vuitton."

Ashley's desire to launch a boutique started several years ago, an outgrowth of her experience in retail sales. Knowing she'd have to have an excellent credit rating to go into business for herself, she applied for, and received, ten bank credit cards. She charged on each card and paid the bills promptly. Before long the banks were upping her credit limit. To keep herself dressed in the finest as well as to make her credit card payments, Ashley was soon working two, then three, jobs. Although she was always tired, she didn't mind because she felt she was making progress toward her goal.

Her live-in boyfriend objected, however, because she was never home, and when she was there, she was pooped. Their relationship deteriorated, both emotionally and sexually, and he moved out. Devastated and exhausted, Ashley fell apart. She sank into a depression so severe that she couldn't work, couldn't eat. She lost thirty pounds in a few weeks. "I didn't want to kill myself," she says, "but I didn't want to live, either." She eventually pulled out of her depression with the help of many friends, but by then she had been off work for two and a half months and was hopelessly behind in her payments. To catch up she started selling things, and soon her apartment was stripped and she was out of money—and solutions. Finally, she filed bankruptcy to wipe out her eighteen thousand dollars of debt.

Ashley is still working two jobs to pay off a few remaining bills and support her expensive tastes. Her tastes haven't changed, but Ashley feels more at peace now than she has in a long time. She pays cash for everything—she can no longer get credit—and consequently has learned to postpone or do without things she dearly wants. When she postpones buying an item, she tells herself that "something else will come along, or if it's meant to be, the item will still be there when I can afford it." No longer quite so obsessed with material things, she continues, "People get so caught up in money and things that they can lose their health. So now I stop and notice nature—flowers, trees, leaves—and I really enjoy each minute."

Whether or not Ashley can remain debt free I think is questionable. She still hasn't dealt with her unwavering need to always have the best. It's something she learned from her father, and her self-esteem is deeply connected to his approval. Ashley may have modified her priorities, but her father has not. The only way she can get his approval is have all the trappings of success; that's how he measures people, including his own daughter. To stay out of debt Ashley is going to have to do some internal work on these issues so that she can like herself, whether or not she owns the best and regardless of her father's approval.

ANCIENT CUSTOMS

Although widespread affluence and free time are relatively new to American women, women and shopping have a long history. For as long as there have been personal, household, and ornamental things to buy, women have been game. Even hundreds of years ago shopping meant far more than a quick trip to the local bazaar or marketplace to pick up some necessity. Shopping has always been rife with opportunity: a chance for women to take a break from the numbing monotony of their everyday chores, an opportunity to get out of those grungy work clothes and put on a clean dress and get out of the hut, hovel, or house. It also provided an occasion to be around people, to have someone to talk with.

Shopping took on new meaning with the onset of the Industrial Revolution before the Civil War, when manufactured goods started to become readily available. This period reinforced the role of women as the chief consumers of the middle class. It was also during this time that department stores made their debut. For the first time, many different items were available under the same roof, and eventually some of the smaller specialty stores disappeared. Department stores during the late 1800s and early 1900s were sumptuous places that offered more than goods for sale. There were luxurious waiting rooms, art galleries, and writing rooms, where the daily newspaper was also available. Some stores even had restaurants that served ladies' luncheons. This pairing of shopping with eating was the precursor of our contemporary custom of getting together with friends to have lunch and go shopping. Shopping thus became an unstructured form of leisure that took little advance planning and was socially acceptable.

When women began shopping in earnest during this period, they also got a taste of power—the potency that came from making decisions and having money. Imagine how satisfying that must have felt while living day in, day out in a culture where men not only made all of the important decisions but held the money as well. Men were in charge, and women had to find ways to adapt to their repressive environments. I suspect that one way they coped was by learning to work around their husbands, since direct confrontation was out. A vivid picture of marriage during this period comes from *The Light of the Home: An Intimate View of the Lives of Women in Victorian America* by Harvey Green and Mary Perry:

"The husband's obligation was to love and cherish his wife, but this behavior was paradoxically linked to *her willingness to submit to him cheerfully in all areas of life*" (italics added).

For example, if a woman wanted to buy her son a special marble, or if she wanted a new calico dress, she had to get her husband's approval. If he said yes, then everything was dandy. If he said no, his wife had two alternatives: either cave in to his wishes or plot how to get her own way. If she decided on the latter course, then pennies and quarters had to be squirreled away to purchase the forbidden item. Next she had to figure out a way to sneak away to the store and buy it. Then she had to spirit it home and tuck it away somewhere in the house until the time seemed right to bring it out.

So, until quite recently, women had to follow a set of rules as constricting as a whalebone corset. While men could rage, storm, and bluster, women could not. To do so would fly in the face of their chief marital responsibility—to please their husbands. Once again women had to go underground and express any negative feelings in acceptably feminine ways. When angry they grew quiet, withdrew sexually from their husbands, dreamed of revenge, and made clandestine trips to the local emporium.

Women have radically improved their lives in the last fifty years or so, but many still feel connected to these antiquated rules. Pat's sense of triumph when she pulls one over on her powerful and controlling husband is not only rooted in the dynamics of their relationship; it is also a carryover from centuries of adapting to powerlessness.

THE SHOPPING EXPLOSION

Although many women have seized more control over their lives, they still live in deeply troubled societies. That's why experts believe that 80 percent of the American population is addicted to something—drugs, booze, smoking, gambling, exercise, TV, eating, or shopping. But shopping is different from most other addictions, except exercising, in that our culture ecstatically endorses it. Buying is perceived as good and exciting. It's something to be proud of, to talk about, even to discreetly brag about.

While the credit card phenomenon is only thirty years old and the automatic cash machine fifteen years old, each has made its own contribution to reckless spending. We can get credit cards by the dozen, and our checking accounts now come with automatic overdraft protection so that we no longer have to bother with making sure our out-go matches our income. If we want something and don't have the money in the bank, magically the bank whisks the money into our account enabling us to capture our latest whim. So banks, former bastions of fiscal conservatism, now promote deficit spending—while they neatly pocket the 12- to 20-percent interest.

Deficit spending is a vague but civilized-sounding term. There's nothing tacky or confrontative about it, unlike "going into debt," "irresponsible," or "in over your head." In fact, the expression somehow implies deliberation or a plan. This is the obscuring term our government has adopted to explain *its own* monumental overspending. Our leaders puff and bluster about it every few months, saying, "We've got to get serious about this," but they don't stop. They just keep overspending at a set amount each year and brag that they've got things under control. Thus, many of society's largest and most influential institutions—federal and state governments, corporations, and banks—overspend *as a matter of policy*. What might be perceived as merely a women's problem is, in fact, a far broader problem. No wonder we run up our insignificant little Visa cards every month!

Recent studies have concluded that chronic shopping has reached epidemic proportions. For example, University of Illinois Professor Thomas O'Guinn terms Americans' shopping behavior a "national problem." The *Wall Street Journal* concurs, stating that it is an epidemic that has taken on a life of its own. Neiman Marcus and American Express commissioned a study of American attitudes toward shopping, which found that Americans enjoy shopping as much or more than watching TV or going to the movies. Seventeen percent of Americans, and four times as many women as men, said they prefer shopping to sex. In another study, by psychologist Georgia Witkin, approximately one-fourth of all the women she questioned—single, married, and widowed—said they use shopping as a "quick fix" for problems. Divorced women, she found, shop even more. If the figures from this survey are extrapolated to *all* women in this country, it means that fifty-nine million American women use shopping as a way of dealing with psychological problems or anxieties.

The Roper organization's numbers are higher. Fifty-one percent of its respondents said they cope with stress by shopping. John Robinson, a professor of sociology at the University of Maryland, concluded in a recent article that "the time spent shopping is way more than the hours adults spend gardening or reading books, the ten minutes or less they spend on sports or the forty minutes they spend playing with children (per week)." *Prevention* magazine's findings state that "compulsive shoppers and people who handle their problems through shopping number in the millions." Last, Robert Cialdini, a psychologist and teacher at Arizona State University, concludes that "people are going into debt at incredible levels without making rational decisions about how and why they are spending money. There is a kind of mindless character to it." The evidence is abundant that you and I are not alone on this. The questions, then, are, what is it about our culture that causes millions of us to stumble to the nearest store for retail therapy? What can we do to stop ourselves? And where, as we stop to scratch our heads and wonder, did all of this spending begin?

The Origins of Chronic Spending: An Informal History

When the United States joined the Second World War, not only were individuals and families affected, but our culture changed as well. As more and more men left to fight the war, millions of women went to work outside their homes for the first time in their lives, making the armaments of war in factories, plants, and shipyards. The war lasted just long enough for women to make a number of discoveries. First, as many women became the head of the family, they discovered that they liked this role. They liked making decisions, and they enjoyed the power that went along with being in charge. For the first time in their lives they also made their own money and decided just how it should be spent.

These new responsibilities and work opportunities brought women independence that would forever change the balance of power between the sexes. When men returned home from the war, many weren't particularly enchanted with the changes they saw in their wives. Psychologically battered, they longed for the comfortable routines they had left behind, but instead they faced enormous readjustments. Many marriages could not survive the changes; couples began divorcing in record numbers. Over time divorce became an acceptable option rather than a disgrace, and the two-parent family ceased to be the strict norm. When couples stayed together, the wife often continued working, which became the genesis of the two-income household.

The war brought about other changes as well. Returning veterans were able to go to college on the newly instituted G.I. Bill, which paid students' tuition and living expenses while they were in college. This meant that a whole generation of men were now able to go beyond high school and get advanced degrees. This, in turn, led to higher salaries and a whole new class of more affluent people, who passed their love of the "good life" onto their children. The war, as well as the space race, led to new technologies and inventions that shaved hours off of household work. Women who did not work soon faced a new challenge—what to do with their free time.

One invention in particular, television, gave people all sorts of ideas about what to do with their lives, time, and money. Programs such as "Ozzie and Harriet," "Donna

Reed," and "Leave it to Beaver" beamed highly idealized and unrealistic pictures of family life into Ameican homes. Unconsciously, people grew uneasy and dissatisfied. *Their* family lives bore little resemblance to those fictionalized ones—families that managed to handle crises with grace and humor, whose homes were not only impeccable but boasted the luxury of live-in maids and cooks, whose mothers and fathers were rarely tired, cross, or at odds with each another. And, the commercials sandwiched between these episodes promoted still more dissatisfaction, because subtly the message was delivered that owning things brought happiness. Nonetheless, people were enchanted with television, and they became so mesmerized by it that family members were soon spending many more hours glued to the tube than they ever had talking to one another.

Yet, on balance the fifties was a tranquil time in comparison to the war-torn forties and the disenchantment of the sixties. Values, expectations, and roles were clear. The country was recovering from a war in which good and bad and heroes and villains were easily distinguished. Our two postwar presidents, Truman and Eisenhower, were solid, even heroic, people. Formulas for happiness and a prosperous life were clearly understood. One worked hard, saved money, eventually bought a home, had children, perhaps went to church, played bridge and canasta with other couples on the weekend, and joined service and volunteer organizations. People were also "other-directed," which meant they relied heavily on what other people thought. This, in turn, led to a fairly homogeneous and conforming population. People didn't say what they *really* thought or felt because it might not be acceptable. And being acceptable—as measured by one's neighbors and community—was terribly important. As we will see, this kind of repression, coupled with growing materialism, laid the groundwork for the addiction that hit full force in the eighties.

But first came the sixties, when hippies, a highly vocal and educated minority of our population, protested our growing involvement in Vietnam and invited us to "make love, not war." When the war finally ended, and later President Nixon resigned in disgrace, the country was shaken. Into the abyss stumbled two well-meaning presidents, Ford and Carter, who were unable to stop rocketing inflation or prevent the avalanche of credit cards that banks and stores let loose on consumers. During the seventies obtaining credit was a cinch; one didn't have to do a thing. Unrequested credit cards just showed up in the mailbox, and Americans had a marvelous time buying whatever they wanted. Personal indebtedness soared, and finally a worried Congress passed a law making it illegal to mail unsolicited credit cards to consumers. But by then the damage was done. Americans were hooked on credit, while at the same time, women were unhooking themselves from the ropes of repression.

Burning Bras

The women's movement caught society's changing winds and sailed into our lives, leaving more opportunity and further confusion in its wake. Dissatisfied with their second-class status at work and at home, women rebelled. Those with jobs demanded equal opportunity for advancement as well as equal pay for equal work. Women working in the home demanded recognition and even pay, for the thirty-odd jobs they performed in service to their husbands and children. Women have gotten some of their wishes, as well as some unforeseen problems. Single career women are stressed and frustrated when their careers don't keep pace with those of equally talented men, and women with families are often torn apart trying to fill the commitments of two jobs. At the same time, women who choose to remain at home are often isolated and lonely and wonder if they're underachieving.

Baby Boomers

Children born after World War II are now adults, a majority of them headed into middle age. Many are so highly educated, career oriented, ambitious, perfectionistic, narcissistic, driven, and materialistic that they have earned the name "Yuppies." Because our culture has always revered its youth and followed its lead, Yuppie values have become the norm. The editor of *Harper's,* Lewis Lapham, characterizes America's new civil religion as the worship of money and status. He states that "affluent America never seems to have enough. There is never enough money, never enough love, never enough time, houses, tennis balls, orgasms, dinner invitations or nuclear weapons to satisfy the appetite of the greedy and the ego-obsessed."

In order to get all the things we want, we've had to make a trade, and what we've exchanged is the family. Most American families are no longer able to perform their basic functions, which are to meet the dependency needs of the children and the emotional needs of the adults. Working parents are absent or they are too busy and exhausted to give their children the attention they need. So these children, these so-called Yuppie Puppies, learn to nurture themselves. Given generous amounts of spending money by their parents— $4.73 billion to children between ages nine and twelve and $78 billion to teenagers—the kids follow their parents' example when they have time on their hands and money to burn. They head for the malls, their home away from home. There they go to the movies, check out shops, scrutinize the opposite sex, eat junk food and pizza, rendezvous with forbidden lovers, or just cruise.

Teens not only spend prodigious amounts of their own money; it seems that they and their older siblings also directly influence their parents' spending to the tune of $40 billion a year. Half of all teenage girls shop weekly for family groceries, and they buy the brands of food *they* like, not necessarily what their parents would choose. Accordingly, Kraft now places ads for convenience foods in teen magazines, such as *Seventeen*, and Kellogg's has brought out a new cereal aimed expressly at teens. Teenagers also shop for clothes with the "right" labels, a fact that was demonstrated so clearly by the obsession several years ago with designer jeans.

The interest in labels now begins when the child is quite young, about two years old, and is in full bloom by the age of six, according to Dale Wallenius, publisher of the *Market to Kids Report*. Marketeers, previously reluctant to pander to toddlers and young children (except for cereals and toys), have overcome their scruples as kids' power became apparent. Recently Sony introduced a "My First Sony" line of audio products for children four and up. For Christmas giving, Fisher Price introduced its $225 kiddie video camcorder. Children can keep track of their busy schedules in adult-size agenda books that are fast sellers at Bloomingdale's.

Sociologists conclude from all of this that the family has changed from being child-centered to child-run, a shift that is mainly caused by the fact that both parents must work. Parents cede power on many fronts, from television viewing and restaurant selection to clothes shopping and vacation planning. Children also have become active participants in which home computers to buy, and they have definite preferences in appliances.

When a whole generation of children act and are treated as autonomous mini-adults, these children are inevitably shortchanged. Jane Healy, author of *Your Child's Growing Mind*, points out that it's during childhood that the brain's neurological connections are formed, in part through rough-and-tumble exploratory play. When that kind of play is bypassed in the rush to maturation, kids lose certain reasoning abilities. Healy tells the story of an outing she had with preschool boys. When the boys came to a log blocking their path, they were at a loss as to how to continue their walk. It didn't occur to them to climb over the log. "Children need time to ponder, and we don't give them time anymore," Healy concludes. "Children are becoming more sophisticated as consumers, but less experienced at being children."

What Healy says about our children is precisely true of the adults in our culture. In our rush to secure achievement, acceptance, success, and status, we're no longer comfortable with just *being*. We've lost our ability to enjoy and savor our thoughts, feelings, and sensations. When we are quiet and still, anxiety seeps in because we have repressed so many feelings that when we take the time to look inside ourselves, there's a lot we want to avoid. The best way to avoid feelings is to feel nothing. So many of us rush to the stores to escape our emptiness, and we pay twice over as our despair and indebtedness deepen. In the next chapter we'll see how cunning retailers cater to our vulnerabilities and to our need to fill up the empty places in our lives.

Chapter 2

Retail Seduction

Eve's battle with shopping began right after the birth of her first child. She had gained forty extra pounds during her pregnancy and could not seem to lose them. Nor could she get into any of her old clothes. Depressed and panicky, she bought *anything* she found becoming and developed an attitude that said to hell with the cost. She battled these same forty pounds for six years and shopped compulsively to compensate for her demolished self-esteem.

During this time she and her successful husband, Chris, moved from southern California to the northern part of the state. Eve was homesick, angry about having had to move, and found it hard to make new friends. When she became pregnant the second time, she gave up fighting her weight and decided she would diet after the new baby was born. She followed through and joined Weight Watchers. Meetings were held all over town, but Eve decided to go to the one that met in the basement of a major department store. She steadily lost weight and vividly recalls passing through the store on the way to her meetings, stopping to admire herself in two particular full-length mirrors. She would look in the first one and see her new, slimmer self, but she couldn't quite take in her changed appearance. She'd stop at the second mirror just to make sure it was true.

After the meetings she headed upstairs to check out the clothes she had spotted on the way down and she always bought at least one item. When she lost thirty-eight pounds she celebrated with a whole new wardrobe. Today her weight problem has vanished, but her shopping addiction has not. Ten thousand dollars in debt, she pays each charge card down $200 a month and then runs them right back up to their limits. She has merely traded in one addiction for another, for Eve's underlying emotional problems had never been addressed.

Eve's story is familiar but has an interesting twist— Weight Watchers meetings at a department store. It's a clever idea. Get women into the store at least once a week, and they'll be sure to buy something—probably lots—if their self-esteem also resides in the bargain basement.

Stores and malls have seduction down to a science. First, last, and always, their goal is to get us onto their turf and then keep us there as long as possible. It's a flat-out, statistical reality that the longer we stay, the more we spend. I'm sure someone has figures that go something like this: "Keep 'em in the mall for one hour, and they'll drop X number of dollars." Just how much we *do* spend in shopping centers on retail purchases (not counting boring car stuff) is no secret. In 1986 the American public spent one trillion dollars, 54 percent of it in shopping centers. Shopping centers want our business—badly. Astute enough to notice that most American families are short on time and even shorter on ideas on how to entertain themselves, retailers have cheerfully stepped into the void to make our lives more convenient and interesting.

Warren Chaumont, former marketing director for one of

the spectacularly successful Hahn chain of malls that dot the country, said in an interview, "The Shopping Center (or mall) has replaced the town hall or the city square and people feel like they own the malls, that they're public property." Mall owners like that proprietary feeling and do their best to offer us anything we may want. As Chaumont put it, "We want to appeal to all the senses." That's why millions of dollars are spent to make malls look attractive, fresh, and alive with majestic trees, exotic and fragrant flowers, ponds, waterfalls, and sunshine pouring through artfully placed skylights. When our stomachs and taste buds demand satisfaction, there is everything available from conscience-appeasing health foods to burgers and chocolate chip cookies. Bored or tired of shopping (momentarily, of course)? Then rest your weary bones on a comfy bench next to a soothing fountain and let the strolling musicians, mime, choral group, or rock band entertain you. Want to escape a little? Well, at the end of the mall you can choose from several first-run movies. Or maybe you want to "get physical"—so check your parcels, shed your shoes, and go roller-skating or ice-skating. If you fall down or break your glasses, there's a doctor two shops down and an optometrist across the way who can fix you up with new glasses in an hour or so.

Malls are even open when they're closed. There is one a couple of miles up the road from where I live in northern California that offers "mall walking" to people before the stores officially open. At nine o'clock sharp each morning about forty to fifty older men and women stride briskly through the center for an hour (this mall has hardwood floors, which are easy on the legs and feet). They love it. It's safe and there are no weather problems, exhaust fumes, muggers, or snarling dogs. After hours, the same mall periodically offers glamorous evenings of dining and dancing, with music provided by the local symphony.

Experts predict that malls will take another turn between now and the turn of the century by becoming full-blown entertainment centers. One in Alberta, Canada, is a harbinger of what's to come. It was built in three stages, with 850 stores, 110 restaurants, a 360-room hotel, a re-creation of New Orlean's Bourbon Street, a small zoo, an 18-hole miniature golf course, and a 600-foot water slide.

Already on the drawing boards in other locations are plans to cater to his-and-her addictions: sports arenas encircled by boutiques and shops. The Edward DeBartolo Corporation is building an 8,000-square-foot shopping complex right next door to the Superdome in New Orleans. The San Francisco Giants baseball team loathes its windy stadium, and its owners are planning to leave town for another location. Santa Clara, an enterprising little community south of San Francisco, is hoping the dissatisfied Giants will move there, and, as bait, is offering a windless stadium and a shopping center all in one. In a realistic, but blatantly chauvinistic, statement a city official said, "*People* can go to a baseball game, and the *wife* can go shopping."

Stores are laid out with the same forethought as a general drawing up battle plans. Items with the highest markups are located just as you walk inside a store, and each area of a store is planned to produce so much money per square foot. Quick-moving, high-priced little impulse items are placed in key traffic areas to trap shoppers, and at these locations designers go all out to make exciting visual presentations. Have you ever noticed that a department store has an "official" cosmetic department plus smaller cosmetic counters in other parts of the store? That's so the store will have two or three opportunities to snare you with lucrative perfumes and cosmetics. In the Macy's near me, one of these little cosmetic outposts is located on the second floor at the intersection between upscale designer wear and funky sports clothes. There's a small counter with several little stools, and it's a great place to flop down when you're tired or waiting for a friend. The young saleswomen are sweet and perky, and they are trained to be accommodating. They will let a shopper park her heavy bags behind the counter so she may continue shopping unhampered, or if she just wants to rest, she can sample as many perfumes as she wishes. The attitude there is one of fun, not pressure to buy, and I imagine this is deliberate.

Down the mall from Macy's is *the* quintessential department store in Silicon Valley, Nordstrom. The emphasis in this gorgeous mecca is on friendliness and service, which experts say is the coming trend for the nineties. Like everything else, retailers have statistics on what percentage of customers are greeted when they enter a store, the average being 20 to 30 percent. One mall administrator states that successful malls in the 1990s will look at today's percentage and laugh. "It's inexcusable for someone to walk into a store and not be greeted. It's the kiss of death," he concludes. Why? Because shoppers want to feel acknowledged and significant. Many a shopaholic mentions the sense of importance she gets from the salespeople, and store managers recognize this need. They are also aware that shoppers may be lonely, so salespeople are encouraged to remember customers' names and to establish quasi-friendships with them.

But let's return to Nordstrom and its outstanding service. I suspect that the motive behind the store's legendary accommodation is that it wants to make shopping *easy*. If a shopper is lugging around a bunch of packages, a salesperson will walk up and offer to tuck the packages away in a safe place. If a clerk knows you're headed toward your car, he or she will carry your packages out for you. If you buy something, whether on sale or not, you can return it next week or next year without a receipt and the store will still take it back. Eve, the shopaholic depicted at the beginning of the chapter, periodically swears off her Nordstrom card and tries to ruin it by sticking it in the freezer. It doesn't work, because later she microwaves it back to life. But even before her card is resurrected she doesn't have any problem charging, because Nordstrom simply asks for her driver's license number and lets her charge whatever she wants.

A couple of years ago I bought a pair of lizard-skin loafers at a Nordstrom store four hundred miles from home. I wore them about twenty times, and then my feet started growing and shrinking at the same time (see chapter 8 for more fascinating details), and the shoes got so big that I just walked out of them. Undaunted, I returned the shoes to the local Nordstrom and told them my tale of woe. The sales clerk took them back and gave me 50 percent credit. Stories about Nordstrom are standard cocktail chatter, with people playing "Can you top this?" Before you get the idea that Nordstrom slipped me a cashmere sweater under the counter to write this chapter, let me get to the point. In most urban areas, people feel alienated, anonymous, lonesome, and vaguely unimportant. This store treats *everyone* like its most valued customer, and shoppers swagger out with their self-esteems singing and their charge cards exhausted; but it's such a treat, they don't mind paying top prices. Where else can they get an instant shot of warmth and self-importance?

THE PSYCHOLOGY OF SALES

Most of the women interviewed for this book were not particularly drawn to sales, but those who were talked about them with a fervor bordering on religious zeal. The word that popped up most often when they discussed sales was *challenge*. They relish getting the lowest possible prices and will go miles out of their way for the satisfaction of saving a few pennies, even if the cost of the gas outweighs the savings. The high for sale addicts is the call of the hunt and bagging the best possible bargain.

Eve, the woman mentioned at the beginning of the chapter, is a bargain hunter. Proudly, she shared the satisfaction she felt when she purchased a Calvin Klein outfit at one store, brought it home, hung it in her closet with the sales slip attached (she does that with all of her purchases in case she changes her mind), and then found the exact same outfit somewhere else for fifty dollars less. She bought that one, too, and then returned the first outfit all nice and tidy in its plastic bag, complete with sales slip. When you examine the motives underlying Eve's shopping habits, her love of bargains makes sense.

Like many other women, Eve shops primarily to get away from the house, the kids, her husband, and *responsibility*. When she shops for a few hours on Saturday and Sunday, it is the primary way she pampers herself. A secretary, as well as a mother of two young kids, the word she used most often in describing her life was *overwhelmed*. The hours she spends tracking down bargains don't seem frivolous to her. On the contrary, it's Eve's primary way of caring for herself. Like other bargain hunters, she also has a nifty rationalization to support her habit. Buying things on sale is seen as a way of both saving money and making money at the same time, since the money saved then becomes money that can be spent.

Retailers also benefit from sales. First, they unload merchandise for about what they paid for it. If they sell something for 50 percent off, retailers break even on the cost of the item, because the markup (called keystone) on most items is 50 percent. Second, they get customers into the store, and unless a shopper is fanatically self-disciplined, she'll buy something else at full price. So the retailer profits, the shopper thinks she's gotten the deal of the century, and everyone ends up happy.

Sales and chronic shopping are, of course, encouraged by advertising. Advertising people know exactly where women are vulnerable, and they use this knowledge to encourage women's shopping habits. Aware that most Americans feel "out" and want to be "in," advertisers capitalize on buzz words that have to do with belonging. Cognizant that women also have a higher rate of depression that is often accompanied by feelings of lifelessness, they promise to bring energy and vitality into women's lives. Our society associates fun with happiness, a myth perpetuated by television advertising. Young, good-looking people are portrayed in states of perpetual motion, laughing, skipping, running, bouncing, tossing, teasing, leaping, and cavorting. The message from these kinetic ads is clear: if we buy these products we will not only beat back depression but have enormous fun doing it.

The following are some ads I've clipped out of the paper, seen on TV, or found in catalogs.*

- "Believe me, clothes that look and feel this good can raise your spirits even when you're grounded." (Target: depressed people.)

- "Outdressing the Competition. It's a jungle out there. Making the right first impression counts—a lot. A lasting impression . . . even more so. [We're] dedicated to keeping you a step ahead: because you can't afford to make a mistake on how you look." (Target: competitive women with precarious self-esteem.)

- On TV: two women are standing in a beautiful green meadow, and one turns to the other and says, "I want to get away and relax." "Where?" asks the other. "Bloomingdale's" is the reply. (Target: anxiety-ridden people who can't relax.)

- "Imagine your friends and family around a beautiful dining room table. After our sale, you'll actually hear their compliments." (Target: women who depend on others' approval for their self-esteem.)

- A picture of expensive living room furniture takes up half a page in the newspaper. To the right of the picture is text describing the furniture, and superimposed on the type in gray, half-tone writing is the phrase "Come Alive!" (Target: millions of shopaholics and addicted shoppers who feel empty and dead inside.)

---

*The interpretations, as well as the analyses of the target audiences, are mine.

- "Discover Shopping At Midnight. Why count sheep, when you can shop? We're the store that never closes. 24-hour-'round-the-clock shopping lets you pick a total wardrobe before you hit the hay." (Target: tense insomniacs as well as depressed people, who generally have problems sleeping.)

- "Thank you for shopping at . . . we value your card-member relationship!" (Target: women lacking in relationships or dissatisfied with the ones they have.)

Addictions require both motivation and opportunity, and every year eleven billion glossy catalogs are mailed to our homes to make sure we have every opportunity to shop. And, we are taking full advantage of these slick little pamphlets that stuff our mailboxes. Sales were $27 billion in 1988, up 15 percent from the year before. In comparison, sales in stores have risen a paltry 5.2 percent. Catalogs fill a need for almost everyone. Busy career women who have no time to shop can flip through a few catalogs while they're wolfing down dinner and pick out their whole fall wardrobe. Women with time on their hands can linger over the possibilities, today considering an outfit from Spiegel, tomorrow considering one from Hanover House. Once a decision is made, all one has to do is dial a toll-free number, talk to a cheery operator, and presto! Two to three weeks later one of those yummy, chocolate-colored UPS trucks pulls up in front of *your* house with your outfit of the week. It's kind of like Christmas—you get a package to open. If you don't like the item, most catalog companies will pick up the offending merchandise at no charge, and you can start over again.

Catalogs are sent out by retail stores as well, because stores that mail catalogs eventually develop strong name recognition, like Neiman Marcus. The pictures also stimulate our interest in what else might be available in the stores, so, of course, we have to run in and take a quick peek.

Shopping by television is much newer than catalog shopping and has only increased in the last five years. One shopaholic, Andrea, wrote about her experiences shopping through TV:

> *If, If, If . . . If I'd never gotten a remote control, I never would have found the Home Shopping Network. There I was merrily switching channels, and I discovered this program that appears to sell tons of gold and silver chains, Italian pottery, and an unlimited supply of cubic Zircons. The amazing thing to watch is how excited the host gets over the ugliest item in the world! That's what hooked me. Just watching people buy these things and get excited about talking on the air. It was fun, and I got a kick out of watching how happy everyone seemed to be.*
>
> *Well, finally, I succumbed, but I only bought a vacuum cleaner the first time. I'm a bargain hunter and it was really a good deal and was very practical. But then I started watching the program almost every night when I got home from work, and so I bought some more stuff, and then some more. I haven't quit yet, but I'm getting close. Visa sent me this nasty letter the other day about my account.*

Another addicted TV shopper, Jane, spends twenty-five hundred dollars a month on purchases from the "Home Shopping Network," according to *Star* magazine. She likes the hosts, too. "I've called up and talked to Bobby Ray, Budget Bob, Susan Jones, and others," she bubbles."Even early in the morning, they are all vibrant. [It's] just fantastic." Jane has three TV sets situated around the house so that she won't have to miss a minute of the program, even when she's in the bathroom. She's concluded that the "Home Shopping Network" (HSN) makes shopping easy—maybe *too* easy. But, she continues, "I'm a buyer. I see things and I have to have them. Before it was malls. Now I never go to the malls unless I want to really walk to keep in shape. But I have HSN's exercise bike, which I just love. Now I can exercise while I'm watching HSN."

It's unlikely that many others are quite as far gone as Jane, but approximately thirty-five million others do tune in the show. It's become a couch potato's shopping dream, and the upbeat nature of the hosts and the callers seems to be a large part of the show's appeal.

Supermarkets must be even more aggressive than catalogs or television shopping programs in their approach to sales. Because supermarkets make only about one penny for every dollar they take in, their merchandising strategies are elaborate. Every square inch of the market is scrutinized weekly by computers and managers. Decisions are then made as to what products to buy, where to put them, and how profitable each one is. Whether or not to carry one yellow cake mix from Duncan Hines and another from Pillsbury, or maybe a German chocolate from Betty Crocker instead, is the kind of decision that high-level managers will agonize over for two hours. Other strategies are similarly thought out.

Shoppers, for instance, are divided into four types. First are the "reluctant shoppers," those who hate shopping but know they've got to do it. Second are "dollar watchers," people who see shopping as a me-against-them kind of experience. They are more apt to go to big warehouse-type markets and buy things in bulk. "The pros," on the other hand, love to shop but are aware of price and value. Last come impulse shoppers—called "candy store kids"—who love marketing. A supermarket makes its opening statement in the area near the entrance, which are called the "power alleys." If a store is catering to the dollar watchers and the candy store kids, it will have sale items at one entrance and flowers and champagne at the other. If it's catering to the well-to-do, it will put gourmet foods, lavish take-out delicacies, and party goods at one entrance and the finest fruits and vegetables at the other.

Basic food items, such as dairy products, meat, and vegetables, are placed around the perimeter of the store so that customers will have to walk down other aisles to get to them. Bread, detergent, and other basic necessities are purposely spread around the middle of the store and interspersed with higher-priced impulse items.

Just like malls, supermarkets court our senses. Lighting is designed to draw us toward certain items, while relaxing music wafts through the store, enticing us to stay just a little bit longer. The packaging and color of items are key. Detergents have the macho look—hefty boxes with aggressive colors like red and orange and bold, strapping print. Hand soaps are packaged in soft, muted colors, unless they're after B.O.; then they toughen up a bit with that brisk, outdoorsy look. They're usually green. Higher-priced items reside right where we can easily reach them, at eye level, while their cheaper competitors slum it on the bottom shelves. And so it goes throughout markets, stores, department stores, and malls. Everything's in its place, and that place is somewhere easy to reach. Just like your twenty-four-hour automated teller.

The significance of the information in the last two chapters cannot be overestimated. In some ways, a shopping addiction is much tougher to overcome than, say, a cocaine addiction. Since both cocaine and shopping trigger the pleasure center of the brain, we face similar deprivation when we quit. Of course, the physiological addiction that cocaine causes is far more severe biologically than the withdrawal from shopping. But when a person is addicted to a substance like cocaine, she can check into a treatment center, get weeks or months of professional help to get off the drug, and come out with a clean slate. When released, the cocaine addict will have to resume her life and deal with all of the pressures that led her into addiction in the first place. But at least when she turns on the radio or television, she'll encounter dozens of public service messages that support her quitting and applaud her decision to go straight.

When a woman decides to quit her shopping addiction, her main sources of support must be herself and her family because public awareness of shopping addictions is negligible.

Quitting becomes rather heroic when you look at the twin forces—ignorance and encouragement—that have to be overcome in our culture. Centuries of tradition have declared it our duty and responsibility as caretakers to shop for the needs of our families. At the same time, television, newspapers, radio, telephone solicitors, mail advertisements, magazines, billboards, taxi cabs (both inside and out), buses, and subways all bombard us with messages to buy. Their encouragement has both the seductive quality of a lightly perfumed scarf and the icy precision of scientific research. Turning away from all of this temptation isn't easy. But it's kind of like fending off a lounge lizard. You've got a fighting chance when you've heard all the lines before.

Chapter 3

Evaluating Your Stress and Shopping Habits

Shopping problems take many forms, and in this chapter you will have an opportunity to take several different quizzes to see just where your shopping patterns fall on the continuum. The first test will help you distinguish whether you are a shopaholic or if your shopping has progressed into addiction. Next you'll find a list of behaviors that signal when a person may be slipping into addiction.

If the idea of taking these tests makes you extremely nervous, and you feel like closing the book and forgetting the whole thing, then skip the quizzes for now. As you continue through the rest of the book and discover that there are *many things you can do* to gain control of your shopping, you will become more comfortable with taking a look at yourself. In the meantime you'll find the rest of this chapter both useful and heartening. After the quizzes you'll meet Vicki, a client who entered therapy because she had run up her charge cards to twenty-five thousand dollars. Her first therapy session is presented exactly as it occurred. Further sessions, sprinkled throughout the book, will show how she overcame her addiction. This chapter concludes with a discussion of stress and the role it may be playing in your life. You'll also find a questionnaire to help you determine your own particular sources of stress.

Are You a Shopaholic or an Addicted Shopper?
A Self-Evaluation Quiz

Although each of the following questions should be answered yes or no, space is left after each question for you to expand upon your answer. Circle the answer that is most appropriate.

1. Has shopping become the most frequent way you cope with upsetting feelings?
   Yes   No

2. Do you feel uneasy without your credit cards?
   Yes   No

3. Do you use shopping as a way of making contact with other adults?
   Yes   No

4. Are you and the people close to you—husbands, lovers, children, parents—arguing or having long discussions about your shopping?
   Yes   No

5. Do you usually hide what you buy or lie about the cost?
   Yes   No

6. Do you find that you are not using many of the things you buy?
   Yes   No

7. Are you paying the minimum due on your charge accounts because you are short of money, or because you want to have more money available for shopping?

    Yes   No

8. Do you buy items that don't fit your life-style— for instance, evening gowns or fancy clothes, even though you rarely have an opportunity to wear them?

    Yes   No

9. Are you worried about your shopping?

    Yes   No

10. When you shop, do you get a rush or a high, but at the same time feel uneasy?

    Yes   No

11. Do you spend six hours or more a week shopping?

    Yes   No

12. Do you feel guilty, embarrassed, or anxious after you shop?

    Yes   No

13. Do you spend more than one hour a week fantasizing about what you're going to buy?

    Yes   No

14. Are you preoccupied with thoughts and worries about money, but continue to spend anyway?

    Yes   No

If you answered yes to *three or more* of the following questions: numbers 1, 4, 5, 6, 7, 10, 11, 12, 13, or 14, you are probably an addicted shopper. If that is the case, don't panic. By summoning up the courage to take the test and acknowledging your behavior, you have taken the first step away from addiction. We can't cure anything, from toothaches to addictions, until we acknowledge to ourselves that we have a problem. Your problem is neither hopeless nor incurable. As you will see, many women have overcome their addiction and are living fuller lives than ever before. But your task right now is to let the awareness gently sink in that you are addicted.

Yes answers to questions 2, 3, 8 and any one of the other questions indicate that you may be a shopaholic. That means you occasionally use shopping to fill psychological needs in your life. Whether or not you want to do anything about your shopping patterns at this point depends on how comfortable you are with them. It would be a good idea, however, period- ically to read the "Shopping Self-Check," which will help you monitor your shopping patterns and alert you to any possibil- ity of your slipping into addiction.

SHOPPING SELF-CHECK

The following feelings and behaviors are indicators that your shopping may becoming addictive:

1. Even though you feel increasingly guilty about your shopping, you are unable to stop.

2. You have trouble getting to sleep at night, or you wake up during the night worrying about your shopping and/or growing debt.

3. You are buying more things you don't really want, or are even able to use.

4. You and your spouse are fighting more about your shopping habits.

5. You are unable to pay your bills from your income and are increasingly dipping into sav- ings, your checking account automatic overdraft service, or borrowing cash against your credit cards.

6. You are paying your bills after their due date or are making partial payments.

7. Creditors are threatening to cut-off your credit or canceling your credit cards.

8. You are going to have to get a consolidation loan to cover your monthly bills.

9. You are turned down for credit.

10. Your thoughts are increasingly preoccupied with shopping.

VICKI: AN ADDICTED SHOPPER

If Vicki had had the advantage of the quizzes you just took, she would have been quite clear in her own mind that she was an addicted shopper. As it was, she wasn't sure what was wrong with her when she made her first appointment to see me.

Vicki called one fall afternoon saying she thought she might have a shopping problem. She came in the next week, looking tense and formidable. Slender, with short black hair, she was dressed in fashionable shoes, pants, sweater, and jewelry that was perfectly coordinated. She strode decisively into my office, plopped herself down on the couch, looked me squarely in the eye, and said with nervous bravado, "Well, here I am!"

She then proceeded to say that she had gotten herself into "real trouble this time" by running up twenty-five thousand dollars in credit card charges. Since she was the one who handled the money, her husband, Phil, had known nothing about the enormous debt until a few weeks earlier. Five years before, Vicki had done the same thing, spending ten thousand dollars, and the time before that it was two thousand dollars.

What follows is Vicki's first therapy session. If you've never been to therapy, this will give you an idea of what it's like, and it might be interesting for you to see what, if anything, you have in common with Vicki.

Therapy Session One

VICKI: My husband goes way overboard. He doesn't believe in buying depreciating items—anything that loses value after you buy it. He is so conservative that he would never buy himself new clothes. He'd have to get down to rags, and then maybe he'd buy something. His father and his sister are both conservative, too. Then there comes me . . . the world's biggest spender.

I used to blame Phil's tightness for my spending. I felt that I was getting back at him, and maybe I am in my own way. But I think I had this compulsion even before I met Phil. This is my second marriage—we've been married twenty-five years. This is the third time he's had to bail me out. At this point, I've got him in the hole twenty-five thousand dollars!

THERAPIST: A thousand dollars for each year you've been married.

VICKI: Yeah *(she laughs)*. My husband makes a good salary. We have invested in property, but he says this time if it [my spending] isn't a sickness, or a disease, then there is obviously something else wrong, and I do this because I don't like him. He says if that's the case, there's no point in being married. I can understand his feelings. Why should he stay married to someone who doesn't like him? But I don't know if that's true. I'm trying to hit this from two angles. Last week I went to Debtors Anonymous. I don't think they're going to solve my needs. I do consider them a good backup, but they are not answering my immediate question, though, which is *why?* Actually, I think it started with my first husband.

THERAPIST: Well, let me get some background. This question may sound off the subject, but do you have any alcoholics in your family?

VICKI: No, no. I was married to one in my first marriage. . . . Beyond that, no one was an alcoholic. My father did the best he could. He was in the hotel and restaurant business, and he was gone a lot. What I think I really wanted was for my father to love me. I was very lonely. I think my father only liked me because I was attractive—that was my claim to fame for my father. As long as you did something different than someone else, that was good.

THERAPIST: So your father's value system was based on status, on what looked good?

VICKI: Yeah, that's right, and I'm very much like that myself.

THERAPIST: Which suggests that his own self-esteem was actually pretty low.

VICKI: Right. And, I find I'm like that. I told Phil that I don't have much self-esteem, either. But *he* says, "You do so many things well." And I say to him, "How can you say that? If you could see how you talk to me, how you treat me—you treat me like dirt!"

I know I'm so worried that I shop because I don't love him. And I don't want to admit to him and to myself that not loving him could be the underlying cause. He says to me, "I think you don't get a divorce because you're afraid to," and I don't understand that. Phil says he will take care of me financially for life. I could live my life any way I wanted. But that's not really what I want, I don't think. I don't want to be alone. *(Vicki begins to cry.)* What I did was replace one strong man for another one.

THERAPIST: I want to respond to what you said about leaving your husband. . . .

VICKI: My entire married life has been a battle between what I want, as opposed to what he wants. He could be happy—we kid about it, but he really could be happy with a TV set, being well fed, and [having] just a bed to sleep on. And I really wonder if he would care if I was around. I am very affected by my surroundings. I want a nice home, I want a good car. And yet, how can I argue against what he gives me. I now have a Mercedes with a phone in it. We have a beautiful antique collection . . . that is really, I guess, for both of us. If there's something I want, he will probably get it for me, but I guess it's the little, everyday things.

THERAPIST: Maybe you want more from him as a person.

VICKI: That's right! And he doesn't know at this point if he can give it to me. I think that deep down he doesn't even like women. I can't believe from the way he treats me that he really likes them. I think that something way deep down in his life has occurred, but I don't know what. I think he's a real male chauvinist. He told me a story about a gal he was engaged to once. She used to make his lunch and bring it to his work every day. One day she brought his lunch and he didn't like it, so he just threw it at her! Of course, she walked out and he never saw her again. And when he told me this story I thought to myself, maybe I should have given this [marriage] a little more thought *(she laughs)*. He does the same thing to me, in a way. He says things in front of others that embarrass me and humiliate me, and he doesn't even know it.

THERAPIST: Oh, does this sound familiar. My husband and I have had two major battles about this recently—about how he talks to me. He scolds me, and I'm just beginning to understand what my shopping is about, in part. My husband scolds me and humiliates me in public—not often, but occasionally—and I get *enraged,* and I haven't known what to do about it.

VICKI: Do you keep it inside? Because you're not going to make a big scene about it?

THERAPIST: Well, you see, that's the whole rub. My tendency, because I am a child of an alcoholic and a very strong, and sometimes explosive father, is to calm the waters so there won't be a big scene. Yes, I get mad inside myself. First I get hurt and cry, and then I get furious.

Horrendously angry. The last time it happened, he scolded me at *my office* because I was throwing some stuff in the dumpster that he thought was perfectly good. So a few days later I took all of my accounts and property and changed them into my name only. I went berserk. But what I learned that night—that last time—is that when my husband speaks to me that way, I should say, "This is none of your business. Bug off! I don't want anything to do with you when you talk to me like this." At the same time, I'm also trying not to put so much importance on what he says.

VICKI: But I'm afraid to take that step, to say, "Get out of here, don't talk to me like that," because I'm afraid he will say good-bye and leave.

THERAPIST: Why are you afraid he's going to leave?

VICKI: Because I'm afraid I can't really say to him what I really think without hurting him so much, because I know how much it hurts me when he says things to me. He doesn't know what words will do to you. I certainly don't say anything.

THERAPIST: So it's okay for him to say hurtful things to you, but you're too considerate to say things back? By the way, I think it's untrue that he'll leave. I can't say for sure, of course, but I doubt it.

VICKI: I guess what would happen is that he would get mad at me and storm out, and then come back. I don't know. I've never tested it in twenty-five years. *(She pauses.)* Only now I *can* remember one time he blew up and stormed out. But he came back. Said it was too cold or something that made it okay for him to come home.

THERAPIST: Some face-saving reason.

VICKI: Right!

THERAPIST: Well, we'll get to this. I believe you have a lot of anger at Phil, and a lot of things you want to say to him. Perhaps you say it indirectly through your spending.

VICKI: I think maybe that's it. But if that's the case, I'm in serious, serious trouble, because he feels he can't make any changes or adjustments. Even his parents have said to him, "Now, Phil, I don't want you talking to Vicki like that." And he is convinced he has really improved. So what I have done is try to avoid the circumstances that would lead up to him yelling and screaming.

THERAPIST: Yes.

VICKI: So he thinks he's improved because he hasn't yelled and screamed at me for a month.

THERAPIST: And you've turned yourself inside out like a pretzel . . .

VICKI: That's right. To avoid the confrontation that I know will happen if I stand up to him. If he doesn't like something I'm doing, he wouldn't say, "Please don't do that." He'd say, "Damn it, don't do that!" and it wouldn't matter who was there. And I don't want to put up with a confrontation in front of the other people. The other people don't like it, either.

THERAPIST: Yes, it's better to start when you're alone. But I'm not sure I agree with you about how other people would react if you did it in front of others. I suspect some might be relieved to hear you stand up for yourself.

VICKI: Well, my husband knows I wouldn't do that. I'd just go off somewhere in a corner and cry, or say, "I'm going home." I'd like to just leave, even if we're at an antique show, and say, "I'm not going to take this," and fly home. But I couldn't do that, because I wouldn't want anyone to know. So what has happened is many times I've managed to laugh it off. And I have friends who say, "I don't know how you do that, how you can put up with that."

THERAPIST: One of the things I'll be wanting to discuss with you is the part of all of us that wants to please or impress other people. Other people don't give a damn, but I think it's our pride that keeps us from saying things that need to be said. We think to ourselves, "Aha, they're going to know something is wrong in our marriage."

Right? We're all concerned about preserving that picture, that image, that facade we put up for the people around us.

VICKI: Yes, and then we don't have anyone to talk to about it. I think that's what's bad. If you had someone you could tell, unburden to, you could probably stand it and go through the rest of your life living like this.

THERAPIST: I'm not sure I agree with you. It would help at the moment, but it wouldn't take care of the problem.

VICKI: Oh, yeah, of course. Phil just got through telling me, "Just show me where twenty-five thousand dollars' worth of clothes is." If I say I'd like to buy furniture, other than the antiques [which] we sell off, he'd say that's a depreciating item, so it's not a good idea to buy any. So if I like this coffee table (*pointing to the one in my office*) [which] probably costs $900, I'd have to go to Phil and say, "I've found a table I like. . . . It's on sale for $250." Then I'd have to make up the other $650 out of my pocket somehow. That's the only way I could get that. My husband has made me write letters to my creditors closing my accounts. I agreed, but I only mailed the letters I wanted sent, not what my husband has dictated.

Another thing that bothers me [is] our children. My son is too much like Phil. He talks down to women. He's been divorced twice [himself].

THERAPIST: As you learn to stand up to your husband you will also be helping your son, since he seems to model his marriages after yours.

VICKI: Well, I have to admit, we don't see him that much because I demand a certain amount of respect and I don't get it. Phil has told me I've got to get our son to treat me better! I tell Phil he treats me that way because he [Phil] does, but he say, "I do not!"

The following section concerns Vicki's relationship with her parents as she grew up.

VICKI: My mother was a very loving person, very affectionate, and I think my father was, too. As much as he could be. With him, mother came first and then the kids, and I think that's how it should be. Actually, *he* probably came second and then the kids came third. My father never saw who I was, it was just that I was attractive. He never backed me up, nor did my mother. The three kids were all born eight years apart, so we weren't even really like a family. My sister's a pill, and my brother suffered greatly because of the way they brought him up. My father dominated him. So my brother is now thirty-five and still trying to find his way around. He's in his third marriage.

THERAPIST: So the picture you got of marriage was that the fathers, or husbands, were the kingpins and the women ran around and made apple pies. Men were allowed to get away with a lot—being absent, dictatorial, patriarchal.

VICKI: My father also was a perfectionist—you either hated him or loved him. I don't know if that's why he lost a lot of jobs. My mother and father also had a hobby of fixing up old houses—the houses we lived in. They'd fix them up and sell them. It was awful because I could never bring anybody home. The house was always a mess. *(She continues to talk about the skills she learned from her father that she has used in her home and in her husband's business.)*

THERAPIST: Is Phil appreciative of these skills?

VICKI: Not as much as I wish he would be.

THERAPIST: You may need even more praise from Phil to counteract his criticalness and impatience.

VICKI: I doubt Phil will change much. *It's easier for me to be sick and be the brunt of the whole problem.* I told him years ago what he wanted was an independent doormat.

At this first session, Vicki's situation sounded pretty grim. She was convinced that her husband would never change, and she could not picture herself standing up to him. The idea of separation or divorce scared her. She was obviously under considerable stress.

Some researchers believe that the most devastating component of stress is a sense of powerlessness in one's life. Vicki's feelings of powerlessness showed up in many areas of her relationship with Phil. She asked him to change, and he frequently answered that he could not (wouldn't). When he was verbally abusive in public, she felt helpless to protect herself, because of her fear of embarrassment. Additionally, she felt powerless in determining what kind of home they would live in and what kind of furnishings she might buy. As we will see in the next section, stress is caused by many factors, a feeling of powerlessness being just one among many.

HOW MUCH STRESS ARE YOU UNDER?

Throughout this book you will hear the word *stress* mentioned again and again. That's because stress is the underlying cause of so many physical and psychological illnesses. If a person has a heart attack she is warned to cut out cigarettes and liquor, get plenty of sleep and exercise, and, above all, reduce the stress in her life. That's excellent advice, of course, but it's not always so easy to accomplish, partly because few of us really understand what stress is. We know it's caused by things like being late for work, getting stuck in a traffic jam, waiting for hours for your boyfriend to call—the usual. However, we may not be aware that stress can be caused not just by bad things but also by good things. In fact, stress is anything that requires readjustment. Using that definition, you can see that it isn't just rotten news that's stressful. "Oh, how lovely! Your daughter's getting married," exclaims a good friend. Does the mother of the bride respond with a radiant smile? No. More likely she rolls her eyes and says, "Yes, yes, he's a very nice boy, but my God, the things we have to get done! Do you know a good florist?" So, even the happiest of occasions can have a ton of stress dragging along behind like a block-long bridal veil.

Stress can drag on and on or it can dash in and out, leaving you faint and breathless. Long-term stress, such as living with an alcoholic, can wear you down to the point where you feel like a bent-over bag lady, shuffling through life. Whichever kind of stress you face, it's crucial to understand how it works and where it's coming from, because it, along with patterns formed in your childhood, are the causes of your shopping problem.

About twenty years ago, psychiatrists Thomas H. Holmes and Richard H. Rache assigned numerical values to stressful events and then figured out how much stress individuals could endure before becoming ill. They found that a score of 150 points for events that have taken place in the last year gives you a fifty-fifty chance of developing an illness. A score of 300 or more gives you a 90 percent chance of becoming ill. Unless this past year has been particularly hellish, you might not score in the 150-plus range. Therefore, to gain a clearer picture of the role stress is playing in your shopping problems, I think it makes more sense to look at the stress you've experienced on a cumulative basis, considering the past three or four years rather than just one, to get a sense of the readjustments you've had to make. When Holmes and Rache referred to illness, they meant something physical. Nonetheless, elevated scores can lead to emotional distress and symptoms as well. *Note:* The test has been updated (by me) by adding a few contemporary items, such as kids using drugs, long commutes, addicted spouses, and so on. Those items are marked by an asterisk*, but they won't necessarily inflate your score because the test is designed to allow for the inclusion of additional items.

A Life Stress Scale

Life Event	Value	Your Score
Death of spouse	100	---------
Marital separation or end of love relationship	73	---------

Affair—his or yours*	65	_____
Jail term	63	_____
Death of close family member	63	_____
Personal injury or illness	53	_____
Spouse addicted to substance*	53	_____
Recent marriage	50	_____
Laid off from work	50	_____
Marital reconciliation	45	_____
Job dissatisfaction*	45	_____
Retirement	45	_____
Change in health of family member	45	_____
Pregnancy—unplanned*	45	_____
Surgery—major	45	_____
Pregnancy—planned	40	_____
Sexual difficulties	39	_____
Spouse addicted to process (work, TV)*	39	_____
Discover son or daughter is on drugs*	39	_____
Gain of new family member(s)	39	_____
Business readjustment	39	_____
One-hour-a-day commute*	38	_____

Change in financial state	38	----------
Kids not doing well in school*	37	----------
Death of close friend	37	----------
Change to different line of work	36	----------
Change in number of arguments with spouse	35	----------
Change in number of arguments with child*	35	----------
A mortgage of 80 percent on your home	31	----------
Foreclosure of mortgage or loan	30	----------
Change in responsibilities at work	29	----------
Son or daughter leaving home	29	----------
Trouble with in-laws	29	----------
Outstanding personal achievement	28	----------
Spouse begins or stops work	26	----------
Begin or end school	25	----------
Revision of personal habits	24	----------
Trouble with boss	23	----------
Minor surgery	23	----------

Change in work hours or conditions	20	---------
Change in residence	20	---------
Change in school	20	---------
Change in recreation	19	---------
Change in church activities	19	---------
Change in social activities	18	---------
Change in sleeping habits	16	---------
Change in number of family get-togethers	15	---------
Change in eating habits	15	---------
Vacation	13	---------
Christmas	12	---------
Minor violations of the law	11	---------
Total points		---------

NOTE: Reprinted with permission from Thomas H. Holmes and Richard H. Rache, "The Social Readjustment: Rating Scale," *Journal of Psychosomatic Research* 11 (1967): 213–18.

Evaluation

A score of 150 for events occurring in the last year gives you a fifty-fifty chance of developing an illness. A score of 300-plus gives you a 90 percent chance.

Some of the addicted shoppers I've interviewed have had very little stress in the past few years but are certain that their shopping problems started at a time when they were under terrible stress much earlier in their lives. Gwynethe, for example, a slender woman with long, permed blond hair and jangling bracelets and earrings, has been trying to beat her shopping addiction since she was fifteen years old. Her mother died of cancer just before Gwynethe's birthday, and her father had to take on two jobs to pay her mother's medical bills. Although she was popular with her peers, Gwynethe was acutely lonesome for her mother and her often-absent father. "Money's always burned a hole in my pocket," she states. "First it was shopping and stealing things, and when I got over that I started sewing clothes like mad. I've always spent more than I have."

Other women I've interviewed have had three to four hundred stress points in one year and can even pinpoint to the day when their shopping problems began. That is true of Dinelle, whom you'll meet at the end of the chapter. But before leaving this discussion of stress, I think you might find it helpful to keep this rating scale around where you can take a look at it now and then. That way you can keep tabs on the current stress in your life. If the points start piling up, your awareness can act as an early warning device and you can begin monitoring your life to make sure that you don't add any new stressful events. Being aware of your vulnerability will enable you to make new, productive decisions about handling your current stress rather than heading for the stores.

A more current assessment of the stress in women's lives comes from a study conducted by Dr. Georgia Witkin involving two thousand women across the nation. These women revised the stress values for many life events and added others, like planning a wedding, that weren't on the Holmes and Rache scale. Take a minute to compare how differently women experience stressful life events then when they are rated by both men and women, as in the Holmes and Rache scale.

Women's Life Events Scale

	Points
Death of spouse	100
Divorce	100
Illness of child, parent or spouse	100
Marital separation	100
Death of close family member	90
Personal illness or injury	50
Marriage	100
Remarriage	100
Fired at work	100
Marital reconciliation	100
Retirement	50
Husband's retirement	100
Pregnancy	80
Miscarriage/infertility	100
Menopause	50
Sexual difficulties	80
Death of a close friend	70
Son or daughter leaving home	50
Son or daughter returning home	50
Trouble with in-laws	80
Change in residence	70
Planning a wedding	50

Not planning a wedding (groom's mother)	50
Vacation	30
Christmas	50

NOTE: From *Quick Fixes and Small Comforts* by Georgia Witkin. Copyright © 1988 by Georgia Witkin-Lenoie. Reprinted by permission of Villiard Books, a division of Random House, Inc.

Evaluation

The differences in stress points assigned to life events between the Holmes and Rache scale and Witkin's scale can be looked at in two ways. As mentioned previously, the Holmes and Rache scale was completed by both men and women, and men may have found some events less stressful than did the women, thus lowering the overall stress quotient for many experiences. Men, for instance, have relatively little involvement in organizing the myriad details of Christmas, for example. Another explanation may be that women in the eighties are generally so stressed overall, by the dual commitment of family and career, that some events have become just plain overwhelming.

DINELLE: A CASE STUDY OF A WOMAN WITH A VERY HIGH-STRESS QUOTIENT

Dinelle can pinpoint exactly when it was that she became a shopaholic. It was eight years ago, after her husband was killed in a fire. Left with two young daughters to raise by herself, Dinelle felt bereft of resources to deal with the loss of her husband. In time, many friends drifted away as well. Within a few short months she totaled 243 points on the Holmes and Rache scale. But neither that scale nor the

Witkin's scale takes into account the enormous physical and emotional toll of single parenting. Therefore, Dinelle's score of 243 should rightfully have been somewhere over 300.

That many stress points gave Dinelle a 90 percent chance of developing either physical or psychological symptoms. And that she did. She began shopping more and more, believing "that the way I dressed might attract the right people to me—some new friends—but it hasn't worked. Having lost my husband and friends, I've tried to replace them with things. It's a lonely and insecure feeling."

Even though Dinelle is lonely and uses shopping as a means to draw people closer, paradoxically she uses it to keep people at a distance as well. "Shopping is mostly a social life for me," she continues, "where I can make friends that I can keep at arm's length. They don't need to know anything personal about me—what I have or where I live—and I can choose when to see them. It's a social outlet in which I have total control."

Yet, something odd happens to Dinelle when she shops in big department stores—she has an overwhelming urge to cry. This doesn't happen when she's in a smaller store. Given the impersonality of larger stores, her impulse to cry makes sense. She uses shopping to meet her social needs and probably realizes at an unconscious level that she's not going to be able to make much of an emotional connection in a large store. In smaller stores or boutiques, the atmosphere is more intimate, and sales clerks and their customers often develop pseudo-friendships.

Dinelle's statement about keeping people at arm's length suggests that she was deeply hurt by the loss of her friends after her husband's death and is leery of getting close to people again. So she makes do with superficial and unsatisfying, but less threatening, relationships.

Dinelle's situation is, of course, quite extreme, but I've used it to illustrate the kind of woman who would score at the highest end of the life stress tests. In chapter 4 the origins of Dinelle's need for control will be explored further, because it is a critical issue for all of us with shopping or spending problems. But first we'll look at some new and fascinating research that illuminates what we *really* may be after when we go shopping!

Chapter 4

Blaming the Whole Problem on Your Parents and the Homecoming Queen

Those of us who are shopaholics or addicted shoppers are said to have addictive personalities. This means that when things go haywire, we're apt to deal with our problems by some form of compulsive or addictive behavior. The road to addiction is a long and twisted one that winds itself all the way back to the families we grew up in. Most of the families in question were dysfunctional, which literally means that they did not function properly. Some were in more pain than others, but like all people who hurt, these families had perceptions of themselves, their children, and the world that were distorted. *Their* distortions and false beliefs were part of our daily fare—as predictable as morning cereal—and in time they became our own. Earnie Larsen, author of *Stage II Recovery: Life Beyond Addiction,* states that 98 percent of our behavior is the result of *habit,* not choice. As he puts it, what we live with, we practice. And what we practice, we become.

For some of us, the genesis of our addiction began with our first tempestuous days of life; for most others it came later, in childhood. The following pages reveal how the phases of growing up, from infancy through adolescence, form our personalities and lay the groundwork for our shopping problems.

INFANCY

During infancy we shape our first hazy, but lasting, impressions of the world. We also develop a sense of ourselves, which comes from the way our parents care for us. Let's take the first part—how we form beliefs about our world. Utterly helpless and dependent, we quickly learn whether or not we can rely on people. When we cry, do our parents respond quickly and consistently? If they do, we relax and learn to trust. If they don't, we grow fearful (anxious), worry that we've been ditched (fear of abandonment), and learn to mistrust.

If our parents are negligent or haphazard, our sense of security withers and we grow depressed. In desperation we try to figure out what our parents want. Perhaps we should yell louder? Or maybe if we smile, gurgle, and try to entertain Mommy she'll give us better service. This is the earliest manifestation of the people-pleasing part of our personalities.

Since most of us can't recall the first few months of our lives, it's hard to know what went on then. But if our parents are able to remember, we can get the lowdown from them. I haven't had to do any digging about this period in my life because part of it has always been a source of great amusement to my parents. I was a great big fat baby, with stiff black hair that stuck out every which way, and, I'm told, I had the voice of a truck driver. In the hospital I quickly earned the reputation as the hungriest baby the staff had ever encountered, and I was fed whenever I bellowed. This was a rather satisfying debut, and I'm sure I relished being the star of the nursery, as well as having my every need catered to.

However, things took a decided turn for the worse when I got home. My mother had hired a rigid, Teutonic nurse who believed in a strict feeding schedule and wouldn't deviate from it for a minute. This took place during the 1940s, when doctors believed it was best for babies to be fed every four hours. Period. Never mind when they got hungry. My mother hated the system and hated hearing me cry, but she was intimidated by the old battle-ax nurse.

I suspect that my fall from pampered nursery star to frustrated, hungry baby was quite traumatic. Yes, I would get fed; I could count on that. But my nurse and parents didn't pay attention to *when* I wanted to be fed. I probably got mad as hell and grew anxious. And anxiety is one of the underpinnings of addiction. Another consequence of this experience may be the difficulty I have in getting along with authoritarian women. I instinctively react to them with a you-can't-tell-me-what-to-do attitude.

A far sadder story concerns a depressed, almost mute teenage boy I saw in therapy several years ago. Although not addicted to shopping or spending, Sean nonetheless was addicted—to drugs. His story clearly underscores the connection between our earliest experiences and later addiction. What *form* our addiction takes is an interaction of heredity, opportunity, and chance.

Sean: From Infancy to Adult Addiction

Sean was acutely shy and rarely spoke, so I had a terrible time trying to figure out why he was so depressed. Granted, his father was a little overbearing and given to Irish flare-ups, but this did not explain Sean's unhappiness. Desperate, I asked him to bring in picture albums from his childhood.

His mother joined us that session, and as we went through the pictures she explained that Sean, her adopted son, had spent the first six months of his life in a foster home. The foster family not only had children of their own, but they were also taking care of another infant at the same time. This meant that Sean had to share whatever limited parenting time was available. Worse, it turned out that Sean was allergic to his formula and spent the first six months of his life acutely uncomfortable and crying constantly.

When his adoptive parents took over his care, the allergy was discovered and his formula was changed immediately. By then Sean had been so traumatized that he didn't smile for another year—until he was eighteen months old. This has not been confirmed, but it seems probable that Sean received very poor care, if not out-and-out neglect, as an infant. His depression started when he was a tiny baby, but it stayed hidden until he reached adolescence. Then it hit full force, and he used drugs to numb his pain.

Revisiting Your Childhood

If you can, find out about the early months of your life. Who took care of you? Were you planned or were you a surprise? What pressures were your parents under? What kind of baby were you? If you were the placid, cuddly type, your parents probably found you easy to care for and a delight to hold. On the other hand, some babies are born cranky or rather remote. When their parents try to hold them, they either squirm or stiffen up. These parents worry that they're doing something wrong, feel rejected, and respond to the baby's body language by holding him or her less frequently. That, in turn, reinforces the baby's irritability or sense of isolation.

CHILDHOOD

When parents are troubled, either as individuals or as a couple, their children experience the fallout in one of two ways. Parents who are insecure about their own abilities will put tremendous pressure on their children to be popular and successful—in short, to be what the parent wishes he or she could be. Parents who are dealing with an unhappy marital relationship also may focus undue attention on their children, as a way of distracting themselves from their troubled relationship. All too often, children of unhappy marriages unconsciously collude with their parents by becoming difficult to handle, by rebelling, or by doing poorly in school. Children brought up in either of these circumstances become acutely anxious under their parent's eagle-eyed attention, and do all they can to please, even if that, paradoxically, means misbehaving.

Other parents, especially those with significant psychological problems, are so consumed with their own difficulties and instabilities that they have very little interest or energy left over to parent adequately. Their children are generally neglected emotionally, physically, or both. If these kids are going to survive, they soon learn that they have to reverse roles with their parents and provide both emotional and practical help. To do this they become extraordinarily responsible, because they feel that not only their own welfare but the welfare of their entire families rests on their shoulders. Should they fail taking care of their siblings or parents, they live with the daily terror that their families will simply fall apart and they will be abandoned.

Thirty-year-old Jennifer grew up in a chaotic family, and when she talks about her childhood, I often wonder why none of the horror shows on her face.

Jennifer: Our Childhoods, Our Shopping Habits

Both Jennifer's father and stepfather were alcoholics, and her mother suffered from violent, unpredictable mood swings. When Jennifer's father was home for an extended period of time, the family was terrified because he routinely beat Jennifer's mother. As the oldest child, Jennifer would try to protect her younger brothers and sister by hustling them out of the house and onto the street. Huddled together for comfort, they would hide behind a tree or neighbor's car until the screaming stopped. Eventually, Jennifer's mother divorced her husband, but then she married another man who also beat her, a pattern that would suggest that the mother had also been beaten as a child. In the meantime, Jenny's biological father would appear periodically for visits with his kids—except that he didn't visit with all of the children, only Jenny's younger sister. He would swoop into the house, scoop up the little sister, shower her with gifts and kisses, and then take her on outings. Jennifer and her brothers were devastated by their father's favoritism, and to this day, Jennifer suffers the most excruciating emotional pain whenever a boyfriend turns his back and leaves at the conclusion of a date.

Her unstable mother was dedicated to her job as an executive secretary and was able to control her moodiness enough to keep the same job for twenty years. That was not the case at home, where her violent mood swings broke loose and left her incapable of any consistent or reliable parenting. The task of parenting therefore fell to Jennifer. From age seven on, she ran the household: made out the shopping list, prepared all of the meals, cleaned the house, did the wash, fixed her brothers' and sister's lunches, and got the other kids off to school.

Jennifer is now an extremely competent executive, but she suffers from enormous insecurities. One of the ways she compensates is always to be impeccably groomed and to dress in beautiful clothes, as if her perfectly coordinated outfits could somehow mask the disarray and turbulence that mark her internal life. Her clothes take a large portion of her salary, but to Jennifer, it is worth it to look presentable and in control at all times.

When parents are as blatantly inadequate as Jennifer's, their children develop legitimate fears of being abandoned. In fact, Jennifer's mother often threatened to leave and thus bludgeoned her children into compliant behavior with her threats. Eventually her mother made good on those threats and left for several weeks on two different occasions—once when Jenny was twelve, another time when she was fourteen.

Children who *fear abandonment* throughout their childhood are unable to develop a strong sense of inner security. Instead they are anxious, insecure, and fearful when they are alone. This discomfort with solitude carries over into adulthood. Many women with shopping problems feel emotionally destitute. They seek distraction and attention to assuage their inner loneliness. These feelings make them easy prey for friendly sales clerks who befriend them. I went to the wedding of a shopaholic's daughter recently and was astounded by the guests. Most were owners of boutiques and shoe stores, interior decorators, and florists. These were the "friends" of the bride's mother.

Looking at the situation from a Freudian point of view, stores symbolically become the warm, accepting homes some women never had, and the things they buy become adult security blankets—temporary forms of reassurance. As adults their emptiness is literally translated into energy and feels like restlessness, dissatisfaction, edginess, and boredom. That occurs because they're so ill at ease within themselves.

Parents also intimidate their kids in far more subtle, but still damaging ways. They threaten to withdraw their love from their children if the kids don't measure up to their aspirations. To children this threat of emotional abandonment is every bit as scary as actual physical desertion. Insecure parents are often hypercritical and negative and, as mentioned earlier, focus the relentless glare of high expectations on their kids. Their message is: "Don't disappoint us, or else . . ." Called *conditional love,* the consequences of which spill over onto their kids like an overturned cup of scalding coffee.

Having never received love from their parents for just "being," these children find it impossible to grow into self-accepting adults who value themselves as they are. Instead, they incorporate their parents' critical assessment of them. Their self-esteem is often abysmally low—they feel like marked-down merchandise with a big AS IS sign pinned to their collars. As we all know, "as is" means there's a defect there somewhere. Just search hard enough, and you'll find it.

That's exactly what people with low self-esteem do. Self-consciously they scrutinize their every statement and action looking for how they might have messed up *this* time. Their painful self-awareness also leads to tender, touchy feelings about how others view them; sooner or later they hear a criticism, and their self-esteem sinks even further. Their inner security is also so tenuous that they tend to hang on to friends and mates even when the relationships are unhealthy. This is a result of their fierce dependency needs, which impel them to stick with something damaging rather than face the discomfort of being alone. Besides, they're not sure they deserve more.

Aware that they will never satisfy their parents as they are, children in dysfunctional families either get angry and act naughty or become dependent good children and do everything they can to please. Most fall into the latter category, and as adults they appear to be very conscientious, nice people who don't stir up much trouble. Their unconscious goal remains the same as when they were kids—to please in order to feel accepted and secure.

Pleasing others does *not* come naturally to children. By nature they are self-centered, expressive, hedonistic, spontaneous, messy, creative, and raucous. Pleasing unhealthy parents usually requires putting some or all of these traits neatly aside and relying on massive repression and steely self-control. It also requires something else—a model, or ideal, of how the child thinks she should be. Given enough time, children get a mental picture of this perfect person and then begin their lifelong task of trying to live up to an impossible ideal. That's how they become *perfectionists,* and probably why shopaholics and addicted shoppers showed such a precocious interest in clothes and appearance when they were little girls. Ever intent on pleasing, they tried to present their parents with spanking clean, meticulously dressed little dolls. It was a sure way of gaining attention and praise. Since it became one of the reliable ways of getting needs met, it's easy to understand why it would become a central strategy in adulthood.

When parental love is conditional, kids are aware at some level that they're being cheated of what they see their playmates receiving—love without strings attached. Discouraged and angry, they grow up with a deep sense of having been cheated, and from that comes an unconscious sense of *entitlement*. Because their self-esteem has been damaged, they're not sure how much they dare ask of their adult relationships, and they feel chronically dissatisfied. This feeling joins up with the leftover feelings of entitlement from childhood and the shopaholic or addicted spender turns to the one way she knows how to get what she feels she deserves: she shops.

Another side effect of growing up with conditional love is that that love is often dependent on the child's not expressing anger at her parents. Without a healthy, direct outlet, anger festers. Women with shopping problems have a reservoir of anger that they've never been able to express. Unskilled at expressing anger as adults, they act out their current anger and the remains of their childhood anger in what feels like a safe and nonconfrontational way. They hit the malls.

Vicki (the woman in therapy discussed in chapter 3) learned how to repress her anger from her mother:

> "Both my parents came from European backgrounds, where the man was king. When my father was home on the weekend (he traveled during the week), my mother was able to convey to him that he was the boss, and I don't know how she did that. But Mom was able to submerge her wants that fast!" Vicki snaps her fingers. "The minute he walked in, boom, like that, she catered to my father. Even today I feel very resentful of her, because she will say, for example, that she knows nothing about football. She does that because she wants to make you happy and feel important, so she'll ask leading questions. She also agrees with you no matter what you say. She submerges herself in other people's lives. She's always the one to smooth the waters, because my father has a very volatile temper."

s

...to say that as a child, she was anxious around
...and rejecting father, yet eternally hopeful that if
...tty enough (perfect in his eyes) he might accept

...uch as she resents her mother, Vicki is similar to her in some crucial areas. Married to a benevolent dictator herself, she has given up any hope of having a close, equal relationship with her husband or being treated respectfully. She complies with her husband's orders, buries her fury, and unconsciously gets revenge by going shopping.

Another spin-off of growing up in a home where love was conditional is a sensitivity to *control*. Dr. Philip Kavanaugh explains it clearly in *Pathway to Recovery:*

> Growing up in an atmosphere where being loved is dependent on meeting others' needs . . . produces a child who is sensitive to being controlled. Conditional love is a form of emotional control. Where there is control, trust cannot develop. Conditional love is emotional blackmail, and *when we cannot trust, we must control*. Addiction is the result, because it develops where trust is lacking. The addict seeks satisfaction in a behavior or substance where there is a minimal risk—where she can always be in control.

Charles Whitfield explains the connection between childhood experiences and later addiction in his excellent book *Healing the Child Within*. He says that when we grow up in unhealthy homes, we learn to *repress* our feelings, observations, and reactions. If we should express them, our parents often invalidate or deny them. Let's say, for instance, that a family is sitting around the dinner table and a little kid blurts out something like, "Mommy sure was walking funny when she came home from bowling last night." Well, if Mommy is an alcoholic, most likely everyone in the family will blanch and emphatically deny the child's observation. If this pattern of denial is repeated over and over, the child learns to mistrust her own perceptions and feelings.

Unhealthy families usually have more than just one taboo subject, and the forbidden subjects aren't necessarily as threatening as Mama and her drinking. Being honest, expressing negative or angry feelings, talking about family problems, or even expressing affection can all be off-limits in dysfunctional families. Families in which there is an alcoholic parent are especially riddled with denial. Husbands and wives are loathe to recognize and acknowledge their spouse's drinking problem and try to protect both the alcoholic and the children from the consequences of facing the truth. The children may whisper about it to one another but hide it from extended family members and friends.

Jessica's childhood vividly illustrates how this process works. But before we get into her childhood, a word about Jessica: she is an addicted shopper who spends approximately six hours a day shopping. These six hours become more amazing when you take into account the fact that she lives on an island off the East Coast, where there are very few stores.

Jessica: Shopping to an Extreme

A tall, attractive woman, Jessica has erect posture, a modulated voice, and a gracious manner that quickly conveys her genteel and moneyed background. Born in New Orleans, she was the only child of a prospering young physician and his socially prominent wife. Jessica remembers little of her first few years of life but has been told by her mother that they were happy ones. Then, when Jessica was two, her father contracted meningitis and died a week later.

Before her father's death, her parents had been building a mansion out of town, and Jessica and her mother moved there not long afterward. Although Jessica's grandmother lived with the family, as well as a nanny and a large staff, Jessica was lonely for playmates. Most of the kids lived in town. When Jessica was six, her mother married a man Jessica loathed.

"He wasn't good with kids," she recalls. "He was an alcoholic who lived off my mother's money. He was jealous of me and a philanderer, to boot." Her relationship with her stepfather was painful. She desperately wanted him to care for her; instead, she got indifference. If they were left alone together in a room, neither could think of a thing to say, so they said nothing and sat in silence. Interestingly, Jessica's mother never once discussed with Jessica her husband's rejection of Jessica or his alcoholism. She tried to compensate for his coldness by being a warm, affectionate, indulgent mother.

Every day after school Jessica was allowed to go to the dime store and buy whatever she wanted. Even on trips, the dime store was the first stop the family made when they pulled into a new town. These shopping expeditions were the highlight of each trip, so it's easy to see how shopping temporarily distracted Jessica from the discomfort of being cooped up on long trips with her stepfather. Over a number of years, she unconsciously came to associate relaxation with shopping, a connection that still operates today.

Jessica talks openly about her terribly low self-esteem. Surely her stepfather's rejection played an important role in her forming such a devastating picture of herself. As an adult one of Jessica's mini-addictions is gold bracelets. When we discussed this Jessica said, "I think they help me feel better about myself. Not in a snobby way, but because I'm so uncomfortable around most people. Especially smart people." Perhaps the jingle-jangle of gold bracelets gives Jessica a tiny bit of security and a kind of armor to protect her from the rejection she both dreads and expects.

Jessica's candid description of her miserable self-esteem was almost as painful to listen to as it was for her to reveal. I asked if she had ever considered taking a course at the local junior college—to get her mind off shopping as well as give her self-confidence a little boost. Startled by my suggestion, she said, "Oh, no, I couldn't do that. I couldn't pass a class if my life depended on it." "Once," she confessed, "I thought about getting a job in one of the local gift shops, but I knew I'd *never be able to figure out how to count the change right." This, from a woman who had received a very fine private education through the twelfth grade. It's not entirely believable to me that Jessica could have such pitiful self-regard just from the impact of her alcoholic stepfather. It seems that some other destructive factors must have been present in her family to decimate her self-confidence. Perhaps her mother and the family servants attempted to compensate for her stepfather's rejection by spoiling and overprotecting. Both tactics diminish a growing child's sense of competence and ability to survive in the world on her own.*

Many troubled families are also *unpredictable*. Family members learn that they can expect the unexpected at any time. Alcoholic parents, for instance, and parents who have little self-control, constantly spring unpleasant surprises on their kids. A drunken father may say something outrageous and embarrassing, a volatile mother will explode without warning. Kids growing up in these families tend to be chronically nervous and insecure.

Anxious parents with a shabby self-esteem often *invade* their children's lives, probing and examining their every thought, feeling, and action. The boundary lines between these overinvested parents and their kids grows blurry, because the parents feel and imply in a hundred different ways, "You are me and I am you." Always present is the underlying message that some thoughts and deeds are *shameful*, while others are acceptable and a source of pride. In these families tremendous importance is put on what others will think. "My God, if Aunt Hilda hears about this our name will be Mudd," the disappointing child is told. Or, should she excel, her parents boast to everyone within earshot. Ruth, for example, hated how her parents continually gloated over her every success.

Ruth: Coping with Invasive Parents

A dark-haired beauty with sorrowful eyes, Ruth recalled an incident that took place when she was in the fifth grade.

One day she brought home a social studies paper on which she had gotten an "A." Ecstatic, her parents made a beeline for the phone. She remembers wanting to yell, "No! You don't understand. I did get an 'A,' but what you don't know is that I didn't do my homework yesterday and sometimes I hate school. I'm not all that good." She said that every time her parents raved about her, she felt like a fraud. Children who grow up in invasive families learn to keep their thoughts and feelings to themselves. Otherwise, their confidences are betrayed and their every move blabbed all over the neighborhood. As adults they have a hard time letting down their guard and tend to miss out on the rewards of emotional intimacy.

There are other, more ominous outcomes of parental invasion and boundary blurring. One of the most courageous clients I've ever known (who wished to remain anonymous and could not bring herself to give another person's name to her experiences), grew up in a family in which her parents jointly invaded her body *every other afternoon of her childhood* by giving her an enema. Afterward, she was bathed. The whole, sick process took two agonizing hours. A bright and brave woman, she has not flinched from facing this horrifying period in her life. She not only is in therapy, but attends two weekly group sessions of Incest Survivors Anonymous, a free, twelve-step recovery program for men and women who have been molested. Interestingly, she had never thought of her parents' behavior as molestation until she first talked about it in therapy. Invasion and boundary blurring were simply things she had grown up with.

A few years ago, this woman's parents sent her a tape of one of their lovemaking sessions because they were "afraid she might have gotten negative messages about their sex life." Her parents, by the way, are highly respected in their small community in the Midwest. They attend church regularly, and are very circumspect in all of their dealings in the community. Being well thought of by their neighbors and the townspeople dictates many of their decisions and activities.

So far we've covered a lot of feelings, behaviors, and rules that are common in dysfunctional families. If you are struggling with a shopping addiction, there is a pretty good chance that you encountered some of these dynamics in your family.

At this point I think it would be beneficial to take several days to think and write about how the behaviors in the following list were expressed in your family and how they affected you as a child. Then consider whether or not you are responding to these conditions *as if they were real today*. Most of us do, so don't feel alone. Later in the book you'll discover how you can get rid of these childhood shadows. But for now it's enough just to become aware of how big a role they play in your everyday life.

1. Repression
2. Family secrets
3. Denial
4. Unpredictability
5. Conditional love
6. Tenseness and anxiety
7. Worry
8. Invasiveness
9. Insecurity
10. Rejection
11. Perfectionism
12. Need to control
13. Self-doubt
14. People pleasing
15. Being on guard

16. Fear

17. Boundary blurring

18. Emptiness

19. Fear of abandonment

20. "No comment" rule

ADOLESCENCE

During adolescence the importance of our family recedes as we turn our attention to the next enormous challenge in our lives—becoming teenagers. For some of us, pleasing our parents was a cinch in comparison to being accepted by our teenage peers. Dressed in our back-to-school best, we set out for junior high in comforting groups of twos and threes, excited, self-conscious, giggling. At last we were throwing off the shackles of babyish grammar school and heading for the big time. We didn't know that six years later we'd pop off the other end of the assembly line, bruised and toughened like combat marines.

Of course, not everyone had a tough time of it. In my junior and senior high schools there was a group of girls that sailed through the whole experience, buoyed by conquests and successes. Oddly, they all looked alike. They were pretty, short, dainty little creatures with curvaceous figures. The boys were enchanted with these girls, who were not only attractive but confident enough to actually be able to carry on conversations with boys. Consequently, not only did they get asked to the dances, but they also reigned over them as princesses and queens. Their parents all seemed to have plenty of money, so their size-six bodies were usually well dressed.

The rest of us—the sensitive, late-bloomer types—found adolescence a horror. Part of the blame lay with biology. Just when we had to cope with hopeless, gangly bodies, pimply skin, lifeless hair, menstruation, and other little challenges, our childhood defense mechanisms faded away and left us as helpless as young children. We covered up our vulnerability with stunning bravado, but few of us made it through those years unscathed.

Above all else we wanted to be popular, and popularity was based largely on one's exterior. Granted, a bouncy, outgoing, extroverted personality was a definite plus. But many of us were too shy and self-conscious to look people in the eye, much less bounce. We couldn't change our bodies or our personalities, but there was one thing we could, theoretically, control—the way we dressed. There, we thought to ourselves, lies the way to acceptance and popularity.

In the fifties, any girl who owned stitched-down, pleated Pendleton skirts and cashmere twin sweater sets gained instant superiority over those who didn't. My daughter's generation is even more blatant about its materialism. These kids dress in clothes that have the labels sewn on the *outside*. That way there can be no doubt whatsoever that they are wearing the authentic stuff, not cheap imitations. In an instant they can add up the cost of a competitor's outfit.

We were more subtle about it. Sometimes we couldn't tell if a sweater was cashmere, second-rate lambswool, or, God forbid, Orlon. The only way to tell for sure was to (a) study the seam where the sleeves joined the rest of the sweater. If there were neat little diagonal stitches, it was probably a good sweater; or (b) feel the material. That meant resorting to "accidental" bumps and brushes to give us the vital information. "Yes, it's cashmere!" we'd hiss to our best friend.

If we learned one thing during those six long years of adolescence, it was that the right possessions, particularly clothing, helped earn acceptance. The lesson was imprinted onto our psyches with hot-pink indelible ink. Many of us who didn't have the requisite trappings felt diminished by our humiliating, second-rate clothes. We entered the race handicapped and were powerless to catch up.

Unconsciously we vowed never to be without again, and we've spent the years since high school trying to win a race that ended years ago. But our hearts don't know that. Mine certainly doesn't. I relish my beautiful clothes in a way that only one who has done without can. My clothes don't make me happy, but they do bring lip-smacking satisfaction. So, many shopaholics and addicted spenders are trying to even old scores and boost wounded egos that have never recovered from the terrible teens.

During high school, Julie applied her considerable intelligence and keen eye to solve her clothes problem, and it brought unexpected results.

Julie: Clothing and the Wrong Side of the Tracks

Julie, model slim with knock-out legs, has turned her unquenched passion for clothes into an occupation. She grew up in a small farming town in central California. As in many small towns, the social stratification was as clearly marked as the railroad tracks that divided one part of town from the other. Julie grew up on the wrong side of those tracks, but that didn't slow her down for a minute. She scrutinized the girls who had terrific clothes and decided she had two choices. She could take her summer job earnings and buy lots of cheap outfits, or she could invest in two or three quality things. She chose the latter strategy, and over the years accumulated an outstanding, if limited, wardrobe.

Today Julie owns a lucrative boutique that specializes in designer clothes. She spends about thirty thousand dollars a year on her clothes and happily justifies her expenditures as a necessary part of her business. After all, she says with a twinkle, "What would my customers think if I looked anything less than perfect?" Besides, she further rationalizes, she gets everything at cost, so she's really saving thirty thousand dollars. What if she had to pay retail?

Is she addicted? I don't think so. A shopaholic? Yes. She is also a perfectionist, and she uses clothes to present a perfect picture of herself. Looking "pulled together" is very important to her. This suggests that she has some insecurities, but then, who doesn't? While it costs her a great deal to achieve her look, she can easily afford it. Her business is very successful. She has a full and balanced life and does not use clothes or spending to fill a significant void in her life. Explaining the difference between her values and those of her sister, she said, "My sister would die happy clutching a big, fat savings book. Not me. I'd be happy if I'm loaded into the coffin in three minks—each on top of the other."

Even though our current habits and values seem rooted in the present, their origins actually began, for some of us, as early as our first few months of life. Our day-to-day dealings with our parents played a significant role as well. With them we learned to be "pretzel people"—we psychologically twisted ourselves into uncomfortable, distorted shapes to please our parents. The only solace that adolescence offered for happiness and acceptance was to demand that we be just like our peers. But how could we?

Now we face the somewhat bewildering task of getting to know *ourselves, our* needs, and *our* pleasures. Only then can we begin feeling better where it counts. Inside.

Chapter 5

Your Neglected Needs and Hidden Assets

Excessive shopping is a complex behavior that has a slew of causes. What triggered Vicki to run up a twenty-five-thousand-dollar clothing bill is entirely different than what compels Jessica to shop six hours a day. In this chapter our personalities will still be under the microscope, but the focus will shift from our childhood to the present to ferret out other reasons that we shop and spend.

A QUICK FIX

In her excellent book *Quick Fixes and Small Comforts*, Georgia Witkin examines the relationship between women with fast-paced personalities—women who drive themselves—and their need for quick fixes. Shopping is one of the "fixes" she researched, but the results were not quite what she expected. Before getting into what Witkin uncovered, you might want to take her quiz to see if you have a fast-paced personality.

The Fast-Pace Profile for Women

Scoring: Rate yourself on each question by assigning a number to each answer, from 0 to 2:

0 points = never true
1 point = sometimes true
2 points = always true

1. When the telephone rings, I assume it's a new demand, emergency, or problem for me to deal with.

2. When someone is in a bad mood at home or in the office, I ask myself if I might have done something to upset that person.

3. Even if I find out that I have not upset someone but that she is indeed upset, I am compelled to make that person feel better.

4. I overschedule my life, leaving no time for unexpected delays or emergencies.

5. I make all of my roles equal priorities and feel guilty of one suffers because of the demands of another.

6. Criticism has a powerful effect on me, so I criticize myself to beat everyone else to the punch.

7. I create busy work because I get more done when I have more to do.

8. I know exactly how I like things to be done and try to do them that way.

9. I get upset when others don't do things as well or as quickly as I do.

10. When I get upset because others are not performing as well as I could, I try to keep my feelings secret.

11. I do more than I should rather than delegate responsibility and I worry about how well a job will be done.

12. I feel as if I am wasting time if I don't do more than one thing at a time, like opening the mail while I eat lunch *and* talk on the telephone.

13. I do things the hard way so that I have a good excuse in case I fail.

14. I hate to wait.

Add up your points and divide by two.

0 to 3 points: Even a score of 1 point puts you on the fast track to fast fixes. But at this level, you are not likely to need fixes now.

4 to 7 points: You are already running a daily race with yourself. Data shows you are having trouble keeping up.

8 to 10 points: You are in the group that is at highest risk for fast fixes! You must try to moderate the demands you put on yourself and others.

11 to 14 points: Although you seem to be personalizing others' behavior and perfecting your own, you have probably set up your outlets and intakes enough to survive—but not thrive. It is time to try to bring your score down by reexamining your expectations of yourself and others.

NOTE: Reprinted from Georgia Witkin, *Quick Fixes and Small Comforts* (New York: Villard Books, 1988), p. 23.

What was your score? The majority of women with shopping problems, according to Witkin's analysis, scored in the four to eight-point range, with a smaller group falling in the upper range, eleven to thirteen points. Witkin was surprised by these results, probably because she expected shoppers to be more driven. Although she didn't speculate why this wasn't so, she did suggest that women who scored in the high range may have older children or jobs outside the home, so they spend more time away from home and have more opportunity to shop.

My impression of shopaholics and addicted shoppers is that they are not so much driven as they are purposefully distracted from a quiet, serene life. Their busy schedules leave little time for introspection and even less time for nurturing themselves in ways that meet their inner needs. Nonetheless, they know they need *something*—some form of pampering. The quickest way for a busy woman to do this is to zip into the nearest store and pick herself up a "nummy"—perfume, a silk scarf, some outrageous shoes. Something that is special and just for her.

Beth, whose story follows, *is* one of the driven types. She scored twelve on the test, and it's surprising that she didn't score even higher.

Beth: A Quick Fix for a Fast-Moving Woman

A short, skinny slice of a woman, Beth literally zips through life. Each day is crammed with tennis games (which she plays ferociously), errands for an even busier and highly demanding husband, committee meetings at the three different schools her children attend, weekly city council meetings (she's treasurer), and volunteer work at the local senior citizens center. Overscheduled, Beth runs late and feels guilty about every appointment, but at least her schedule keeps her distracted, and that's the whole point.

Married for the second time to a competitive, dictatorial, and temperamental utilities executive, Beth keeps excessively busy so she won't have time even to think, much less feel how unhappy she is with her marriage. She would like to get a divorce, but she believes that her husband would respond vindictively and not pay child support for their three children. Although she taught school years ago, Beth doesn't want to do that again, and she has no other job skills. Consequently, she feels stuck and has decided to focus her life on her kids and on community activities.

Ever bouncy and upbeat, the only visible cracks in this woman's armor are her impulsive dashes into the local stores. There she scoops up armloads of clothes, signs the charge slips, throws the bags into the car, and speeds off to her next appointment. Her purchases next land in the guest room, where they may accumulate for weeks before she has a chance to try anything on. She keeps almost everything—dresses, suits, jewelry—but rarely wears them. Instead she shows up for her appointments in the same two or three warm-up suits day after day.

But what about the women in the middle, those who apparently *aren't* running around in circles, chasing their tails? What's the deal with them?

I suspect that this group of women is not *outwardly* driven, extremely perfectionistic, or "time urgent" enough to score in the highest range on the Witkin test, but that they are still inwardly tense, overly conscientious, fearful of criticism, and hooked on pleasing others. They too stay busy, but their lives are more balanced, with time left over for things they enjoy doing. Most of the shopaholics and addicted spenders I've interviewed have numerous hobbies that are very important to them. These hobbies are given a high priority in terms of time, and so these women are more relaxed.

Witkin found some other interesting correlations between the various quick fixes. Of all the fixes she researched—eating, shopping, yelling, napping, smoking, drinking, redecorating, cleaning, and moving—it turned out that *eating and shopping were the most closely related.* That means that if you use one fix, such as shopping, there is a 40 percent chance that you'll use eating as a quick fix, too. The good news about this bad news is that you are forewarned. When you begin cutting back on your shopping, you'll want to make sure you don't head for the refrigerator instead of the store.

Vicki, the woman whose therapy we've been following, experienced precisely this crossover. It came almost exactly a year after her first appointment. At that point she was coming in only once every couple of months for a "check-up."

Vicki

When Vicki stopped coming for weekly appointments, things had been going slightly better with Phil—just slightly—but Vicki was dealing with her feelings differently and had begun playing tennis every day. In fact, Vicki and Phil often played doubles, and they were enjoying playing together. Then Vicki injured her knee and had to quit for three weeks. She came in for an appointment during this time, and I noticed that she was plumper. She had gained about ten pounds.

Because it had been so long since she was in weekly therapy, Vicki had slid back into some of her old patterns with Phil. She had given up the assertive behaviors she had used so successfully earlier. "Phil," she declared, "was being an ass," and Vicki was feeling hopeless. Since she couldn't distract herself with her passion, tennis, she compensated by overeating. "Well, at least I'm not out buying clothes!" she commented ruefully. However, she did decide to come to therapy more regularly until she could work through this setback.

The reason that shopping and eating are so closely related is that they are both "taking-in fixes." Women who are most vulnerable to these kind of fixes are those who desire something: love, attention, or recognition. Unable to get what they need from their families or from work, they give to themselves by eating or shopping.

Witkin identifies two additional kinds of fixes groups. In addition to "taking-in" fixes, there are the "letting-it-out fixes," which include yelling and excessive sex. While both sound psychologically freeing, and maybe even a little fun, research shows that uncontrolled cathartic behavior just feeds on itself. Instead of having a nice little yell at our partner, for instance, it seems that yelling just leads to more yelling. Either our partner yells back, then we yell louder, or our partner doesn't say a thing, which *really* pisses us off, so we yell more. But yellers generally are not shoppers. In fact, Witkin found that yelling kicks in where shopping leaves off, in the nine-, ten-, and eleven-point range. When we recall that shoppers are generally rather nice and repressed women, this finding makes sense. If we could express ourselves enough to yell (even though it's not all that healthy), we might not need to shop so much.

The other category of fixes, "use-it-up behaviors," doesn't really work either. These activities—cleaning, exercising, and working—are incorporated to calm down runaway adrenaline. They are especially appealing to women who like to be in control. Anxious when they, or their environment, is out of control, they scurry around trying to keep the lid on feelings and events, and this frenzy produces more adrenaline. So these behaviors are also ineffective.

Witkin's research adds instructive knowledge about shoppers. Some live in the fast lane and lunge for quick fixes to nurture themselves. Most of us, however, are running a different kind of race, a race within ourselves, and we're not succeeding. That's because the racetrack is littered with impossible hurdles—perfectionism, pleasing others and keeping ourselves under control.

SENSATION SEEKING

Therapist Joy Davidson has other ideas about why we may fall prey to compulsive and addictive behaviors, which she presents in her superb book *The Agony of It All*. I find her ideas compelling; let's see how they strike you. Dr. Davidson believes that all people have a basic drive—to seek sensation.

This drive either can be satisfied in a healthy way, which is called *excitement,* or it can be gotten through *drama,* which is often self-destructive. Healthy excitement is always distinguishable from drama, because (1) the pleasures and rewards of an exciting experience always outweigh the struggles, and (2) healthy excitement offers substantial pleasure or concrete reward. Things can get sticky, though, because the underlying drive of sensation seeking also involves a craving for experiences that are not just intense, but *novel.* Since no experience remains novel for long, the original experience may have to be repeated more frequently, or at higher levels of intensity, to get the same feeling of excitement. This *can* lead to addiction. Before going into Davidson's ideas more thoroughly, you might want to take still *another* quiz. This one Davidson devised to help you assess your need for drama.

Are You a Drama Seeker?

Answer yes or no to the following questions:

■ Does it drive you "crazy" when your routine is the same for too long?
Yes   No

■ Are you sometimes accused, in a manner that feels insulting or judgmental, of being "dramatic" or "high strung?"
Yes   No

■ Are you prone to sudden, sometimes unexplainable, eruptions of anger or tearfulness?
Yes   No

■ Just when things are going smoothly, do you find yourself in a fight with someone close to you or faced with a new crisis?
Yes   No

■ Do you wonder if you'll ever be satisfied by anyone or anything?

　　Yes　　No

■ Would you go to any lengths to help out a friend, even to your own detriment?

　　Yes　　No

■ Do you become strongly attracted to men who are already involved with other women or who don't appear interested in you?

　　Yes　　No

■ Do people accuse you of "making a big deal out of nothing?"

　　Yes　　No

■ Do the people closest to you seem to be in frequent upheaval or turmoil?

　　Yes　　No

■ Do you long for career success, but find that it continues to elude you?

　　Yes　　No

■ Have you tried, more than once, to "conquer" or "change" an emotionally distant, troublesome, or cruel partner?

　　Yes　　No

■ Have you ever been a binge eater or used alcohol or drugs to excess, especially when bored or frightened?

　　Yes　　No

■ Do you complain to friends of being mistreated by others, or by "life?"

　　Yes　　No

■ Do you take secret pleasure in breaking social rules or minor laws and getting away with it?

　　Yes　　No

- Does your life seem more like a jumble of unrelated chapters than a whole book?

    Yes   No

- Is passion usually mingled with conflict and turbulence in your relationships?

    Yes   No

NOTE: Reprinted from Joy Davidson, *The Agony of It All* (Los Angeles: Jeremy Tarcher, 1988), p. 12.

If you honestly don't see yourself mirrored in any of these questions, you probably have found healthy, productive ways of generating all the excitement your system demands. But if like many other women, you saw your actions reflected in some, or many, of these questions, it is likely that you now meet your need for excitement through personal dramas. Researchers have found that women's tendencies to seek sensation actually increase over the years, peaking from ages thirty to thirty-nine and declining in the forties and fifties. The change may have a biological basis or may simply come from having gotten the riskiest activities out of our systems at an earlier age.

Carl Jung, a pioneer in early psychology and a contemporary of Freud, used a slightly different term for this drive for sensation. He named it the "drive to activity," and felt it to be so important that he identified it as one of the five instinctual human tendencies, encompassing the urge to travel, the love of change, and the tendency toward restlessness. Marvin Zuckerman, another researcher in this area, found that some people have such strong nervous systems that they are insensitive to low levels of stimulation and can get excited only if the level of intensity is high enough. Such people, he said, demand intense, thrilling experiences to charge their systems up to the optimal level. From the findings of Jung, Zuckerman, and others, Davidson states unequivocally: "There is general agreement that certain people are neurochemically driven to demand greater sensation than others."

Researchers also have found that married women who score high on the sensation-seeking scale are more sexually responsive, are more inclined to masturbate, and are more likely to have multiple orgasms. In other words, they're sexier than the average woman. They are also leaders in groups, and they loathe quiet environments where nothing much is happening. When these women feel isolated, they tend to create drama to liven things up. Women lean toward drama, rather than toward overtly physical or aggressive outlets, because *they have been raised to meet their sensation-seeking needs through either their relationships or their inner emotional lives*. And it turns out that biochemically, a domestic crisis, a love challenge, and a ten thousand–foot parachute drop from an airplane are equally stimulating!

Sensation seeking almost always encompasses the need for specialness, the wish to find one's own unique place in the world. For men specialness seems to be related most commonly to expressions of independence and achievement in traditionally masculine areas of performance—sexual, athletic, financial. For women specialness and excitement become overly aligned with affiliation, approval seeking, and dependency.

Davidson suggests that women who have the highest level of sensation-seeking drive may have been quite special as infants and young children—more active, more talkative, more exploratory. Since special children know deep within themselves that they are extraordinary, trouble arises when a caretaker fails to validate them. This can happen at any time. Since many shopaholics are firstborn children, the birth of brothers and sisters can be enough to dethrone a special child. Or it may be the child's peer group that sees her as less than divine. The consequence of such shattering developments is that these children then face the lifelong challenge of regaining that lost paradise of specialness. In order for the feeling of specialness to be preserved, proof of it must be established over and over.

THE DOWN SIDE OF SENSATION SEEKING

Dramas, such as picking a fight with our spouse, are the outgrowth of sensation seeking, and help us feel alive, excited, and tuned into life at that very moment. But, when our energy and emotions are spent in this way, we become distracted or detached from our deepest feelings and we hide our unhappiness and insecurities from ourselves. Thus, dramas serve two purposes: they satisfy our need for sensation and they distract us from pain. Pain that we need to *feel* so we can change what is *really* bothering us.

At the same time, compulsive and addictive behaviors, including shopping, create excitement within ourselves. Internal excitement is self-arousing; if you follow a typical shopping spree from beginning to end, you can see how the process of self-arousal works. First comes the pleasant anticipation of shopping; then the high of being in the stores and purchasing (often accompanied by anxiety, another intense emotion); followed by excruciating feelings of remorse. At this point, still another form of self-arousal kicks in—the shopper agonizes about how she's going to pay her bills. Often, mental images of embarrassment flood in as she pictures herself having credit denied, cars repossessed, and so on. In just a few hours the addicted shopper creates an electrifying drama, but one that results in suffering instead of pleasure.

The form our dramatic productions take depends on what needs we're trying to fulfill. Women who are lost without a crisis or bored without conflicts and fights are often "fighters," according to Davidson. "Challengers" get off on striving, and excitement is based on a contest that usually involves a man—one they're married to or one they're not. If they're married, the challenge is to manipulate and draw close a remote spouse. If unmarried, a challenger repeatedly will be drawn into love triangles where she tries to wrest a man from another woman. The area between desire and attainment is her "thrill zone."

Problem shoppers are also rebels at heart. They have a constitutionally low tolerance for tranquility, and their excitement is generated on the hazardous turf between action and consequence. Many were brought up in highly controlled environments where they were expected to be good girls. As adults they tend to rebel against their still-over-controlled lives and the high expectations they have for themselves—by shopping excessively. It's the perfect ladylike way to revolt. One day I received a call from a very excited woman named Marilyn, who had heard that I was interviewing women with shopping problems. She said she was dying to talk to me because she felt she had learned so much through her battles with excessive shopping.

Marilyn: The Shopping Rebel

At forty-two, Marilyn is still the quintessential rebel. She sashayed into my office one morning dressed in a white peasant blouse, a ruffled denim miniskirt, opaque nylons, ruffled bobby socks, glittering tennis shoes, and industrial-strength mascara. Breathlessly, she said, "I have so much to tell you, I don't know where to start!" Her story was hard to follow because it was a bit disorganized, but I found it riveting.

Her shopping problems started about ten years ago, Marilyn said, when she was promoted to a managerial position with a medium-sized manufacturing company. The stress of her new job was "awful," and she began shopping to relieve the tension. At the same time, she and her husband, who was twenty years older and Jewish (she was Catholic but had converted to Judaism), decided that the only way to get ahead was to go into business for themselves. Their plan was to eventually open a discount retail store. Over a five-year period they visited flea markets and bought up lots of marked-down clothing. Soon their purchases overflowed their two-car garage, and they rented lockers all over town to hold their loot. They bought everything they thought they might be able to resell, including two thousand pairs of women's shoes.

Marilyn was as sketchy about her husband's occupation as she was about their finances. He handled the money, but she insisted that all of the credit cards be in her name only (she had kept her maiden name). Yet, her husband had access to these credit cards, and he ran up enormous bills buying her lavish gifts. An unexpressive man, Marilyn's husband couldn't tell her how much he loved her, so he bought her presents instead. Unhappy with her husband's inability to show emotion, Marilyn had a couple of affairs. Eventually her marriage hit the skids. She filed for divorce, but it took two years to get through the courts because her husband made things difficult—he was furious because she had left him for a black man. When the divorce was over, she got stuck with all of the marital debts, and soon afterward she filed for bankruptcy.

During this period of her life, Marilyn acted out (rebelled) in many areas of her life. Stressed by work, she reacted by shopping compulsively. Displeased with her husband, Marilyn turned once again to her primary coping mechanism— acting out her feelings—and had affairs. Her decision to leave her husband for her black lover, Thomas, had clear overtones of defiance.

Marilyn has been living with Thomas for seven years now, but their relationship isn't going well. In fact, he's been physically abusive. Undaunted by all of this chaos, Marilyn sounds very upbeat when she talks about what she's learned. "Now I'm finally in touch with myself. It has cost a lot, but in the process I've learned to like and value me. But it's still a daily battle. I have to give myself positive feedback as much as possible. I have a tendency to give more than I get back, especially with men."

Marilyn has been in therapy for a year at Jewish Social Services, a nonprofit organization that offers therapy on a sliding-scale basis. Because Marilyn is so low on funds, she has to pay only five dollars a session. She feels she's gotten a lot from her therapy. However, she pinpoints one event that was pivotal in helping her turn her life around. It happened during the winter prior to our interview, when she decided to *try skiing. Marilyn was scared, so Thomas suggested she try cross-country skiing, as it is easier to learn and less risky. But Marilyn said no, what she really wanted to learn was downhill skiing. She scraped together enough money for a couple of lessons and fell in love with the sport. In overcoming her fears she not only built up her self-esteem, but also found a constructive outlet for her considerable need for excitement. Skiing has become such an important goal in her life that she is now able to save money for the first time in her life. Slowly, Marilyn has been accumulating ski equipment, which is expensive, and setting aside money for lessons and lift tickets. It's too soon to say whether therapy and skiing are going to be enough to help Marilyn begin living a more stable and satisfying life. If she stays in her abusive relationship with Thomas, one has to wonder about her prognosis. However, she is upbeat and hopeful for the first time in years.*

Drs. Witkin and Davidson each have spotlighted some additional clues as to why women overshop. You might want to take a look at your life and see if their ideas fit with what you know about yourself. If you're living a hectic, overscheduled life like Beth is, you may need to slow down and take time to nurture yourself. Or maybe you are giving out more emotionally than you're taking in. Look closely at your relationships and begin measuring them by a different yardstick— one that measures how much love, plesure, and caring you're *receiving*. If you're giving more than you're getting, it's time to reassess.

NEGLECTING YOUR CREATIVITY

Most of the women interviewed for this book filled out rather lengthy questionnaires about their shopping habits, marriages, jobs, families, interests, and hobbies. In their written responses as well as in our conversations, two themes continually reoccurred. First, the most consistent reason women gave for their compulsive shopping was to "find something special, something unique, something that set them apart." This is consistent with Davidson's findings about specialness. However, these women's desire for specialness may be related to another need. I believe that they use the things they buy to project their innate creativity. They do not necessarily shop or dress to *im*press so much as they do to *ex*press.

What led me to this conclusion were the women's responses concerning interests and hobbies. Ninety percent of these women spent their free time involved with either creative or performing arts (the other 10 percent were primarily interested in sports and animals). The following is a sample of their responses to the questions, "What do you do with your free time?" and "What are your hobbies?": dancing, singing, sewing, needlework, decorating, antiques, table setting, photography, art, theater, gardening, calligraphy, painting, floral arranging, crafts, guitar, crocheting, knitting, collecting P. Buckley and Moss prints—the artistic thing, making wreaths and baskets. Although the number of women I interviewed was small, I believe that the percentage of interviewees who expressed an interest in creative activities is much higher than one would expect to find by a random sampling of the general population.

People who are interested in creative activities are said to be "right brained," while people who are fascinated by more precise, analytical activities are "left brained." This left-brain, right-brain theory intrigues not only because it explains creativity but also because it helps clarify why women and men are so different: why men tend to nitpick and be literal about facts, while women may brush over them on their way to the essence of an idea; why men can set the timer on the VCR and women often find it difficult. Or have you, for example, ever had the experience of telling a perfectly juicy and scintillating story to friends, perhaps exaggerating just a tiny bit for dramatic effect, when your husband crashes into the middle of *your* story to get some insignificant and trivial fact straight? They do that because for some reason they think pinpoint accuracy is important at all times!

These annoying differences between the sexes begin at conception. The brains of all fetuses, male and female, are divided into two hemispheres, left and right, which are connected by fibrous tissue. But sometime between the eighteenth week and the twenty-sixth week of pregnancy, the brain of male fetuses gets a chemical bath of testosterone and other sex-related hormones. At this point, two things occur. First, the right hemisphere shrinks a bit, and second, some of the connecting tissue between the left and right hemispheres is destroyed. Consequently, a majority of boy babies bounce into the world left-brain dominant, while little girls tend to be more two-sided in their thinking, enabling their thoughts to whiz back and forth between the two sides of the brain more rapidly.

This, in turn, leads to specialization. Boys and men favor logical, analytical, factual, and aggressive ways of thinking, while girls and women focus on feelings, relationships, language, and communication skills. It also makes women potentially more imaginative and creative. Dr. Roger von Oech, a pioneer in the semiconductor industry, wrote an interesting book related to this subject called *A Whack on the Side of the Head*. In it, he uses the terms *hard thinking* and *soft thinking* to describe the differences between the way men and women think. "Soft thinking (female) tries to find similarities and connections among things, while hard thinking (male) focuses on their differences. . . . Hard thinking is like a spotlight. It is bright, clear and intense, but the focus is narrow. Soft thinking is like a floodlight. It is more diffuse, not as intense, but covers a wide area."

From this information, other studies, and from my own findings, we can conclude two things: women are more right-brained in their thinking than men, and women with shopping problems may be even more developed than the average woman in their right-brain activities and skills. I believe that such women have deep wells of creative talent that they underutilize in their day-to-day lives. Consequently, they may feel frustrated and be without sufficient direction or satisfaction.

For example, Gwynethe, whom you met earlier in the book, has been fighting her shopping addiction for twenty-five years. She has tried therapy, twelve-step programs, spiritualists—almost anyone she felt could help her. While she has learned something from each of these sources, it was not until she and I had extensive talks about her need to begin using her energy and tremendous creativity in a work-related way that she has had success in overcoming her addiction. Previously she worked as a dental assistant, and she was bored and frustrated. To compensate, she has done substantial volunteer work, and in the course of this work she has met people who have recognized both her organizational and creative talents. Through these contacts she has been hired as a consultant to two small companies, for whom she generates creative ideas about how they can become more successful.

When she has completed her work with these companies, she is seriously considering opening her own retail store. What has always pleased Gwynethe about clothes and shopping has been the challenge of putting together separates and accessorizing them in such a way that they can be worn many different ways, each time producing a different look. As she put it, "Anyone can go in and buy a designer dress, but where's the challenge in that? What kind of imagination does that take?" Since she has taken on her consulting jobs, we haven't had much time to talk, but she is ecstatic with her challenging new work, excited about the future, and, she says, "way too happy and busy to think about shopping."

It is from my own experience, as well as from research and reading, that I encourage you, too, to examine your work and hobbies to see if you might be happier if more of your life involved right-brain work and activities. The pay's not too good, but the excitement, pride, and satisfaction are priceless.

Lending credence to my idea that creative people need to create to be happy (and stay mentally healthy) is the eminent British psychiatrist Dr. Anthony Storr. In 1988 he published a book entitled *Churchill's Black Dog, Kafka's Mice and other Phenomena of the Human Mind*. In this tome Storr examines the lives of some of the most creative thinkers of the last three centuries and concludes that

> Men and women who are creatively gifted are char-acterized by a susceptibility to mental illness which is greater than average, but which does not necessar-ily lead to actual breakdown *because creative powers are to some extent protective against mental illness.* Experimental psychology lends some support to this hypothesis. It has been demonstrated that creative people exhibit more neurotic traits than the average person, *but are also better equipped than most people to deal with neurotic problems.* (Italics added.)

However, this built-in immunity doesn't help if an individual isn't working in an environment where she can unleash her imagination and creativity.

Shopping problems generally fall into the category of "neurotic" because the basis of the disorder is obsessive-compulsive behavior. But, don't be upset by the word *neurotic*. It's a fairly old-fashioned term that applies to many, many people, not just those with shopping disorders. Nonetheless, I think we should take the very good news that comes from recent research. As discussed earlier, creative people, perhaps like you and me, tend to have more psychological problems. That's hardly news, since we know that our shopping is a problem. But at the same time we appear to have a built-in immunity that others *don't* have, so long as we honor our creativity and integrate it in our lives. If you feel you are creative, no matter in what way or to what degree, I strongly invite you to bring it into your life. Also, try to begin restructuring your life to include your need for change, excite-ment, and stimulation. Those traits bring a special liveliness to your personality that makes you unique. And it's delightful being special in a healthy way.

In the next chapter we'll look at another source of both stress and joy—our mates—and see how they fit into the shopping equation.

Chapter 6

Men Who Love Women Who Shop Too Much

Don, a lean and tan man, radiated impatient energy from his coiled gray hair down to his twitchy right foot. He didn't move; he struck—first in one direction, then another—around his spacious real estate office, as he kept his penetrating blue eyes locked on mine. When our conversation veered to women's shopping habits, he barked out a laugh. "You're kidding! Well, you've gotta talk to my wife. She's got it bad," he said, "real bad." Amused, he relayed some stories about his wife's shopping habits and then suggested that his wife be interviewed. Accustomed to women's reluctance to discuss their shopping problems, I was surprised when she called that same day, saying she'd love to talk to me, *alone*. The woman was Jessica, who grew up in New Orleans and had such poor self-esteem (chapter 4).

Don introduced us the next day at lunch. Jessica's first words were, "Oh, I'm so glad to have someone to talk to about this. I hate it, I hate myself and I don't know what to do about it." During lunch we talked about other subjects, and then, after gulping down his lunch, Don excused himself. Clearly, he was relieved not to have to get into this kind of heavy women's talk. Many readers may assume at this point that Don is indifferent and insensitive. He isn't. He's a nice man who loves his wife deeply, but he was every bit as caught up in the web of Jessica's addiction as she was. He just didn't know it. First of all, it's hard for most people, but especially spouses, to look at excessive shopping as a serious problem. This is particularly true if the family is wealthy and the addiction doesn't pose a threat to financial stability. Further, by making light of the situation, Don was unconsciously trying to protect himself from the knowledge that his wife was as much an addict as someone who is strung out on heroin. That's a tough thing to face.

Moreover, if he ever confronted her addiction, he might also have to address some of his own addictions. That, in turn, might raise the specter of the acute pain that neither he nor Jessica wants to feel regarding their youngest child, a twenty-two-year-old retarded daughter who lives with them.

HIS-AND-HER ADDICTIONS

Don and Jessica are in what is called an addict-addict relationship. Both are addicted, but to different things. When we think of an addicted couple, pictures of a bleary-eyed twosome hunched over a pair of shot glasses in a seedy bar come to mind, not handsome, well-heeled people smiling out from the society pages of the newspaper. But ours is an addicted society, and addicts don't necessarily look like stereotypes. Sometimes they look like you and me, and they happen to be nice people doing respectable things like working, watching TV, working out, or building models in the garage.

Retired (Don and Jessica are in their fifties) and financially set for life, the monotony of his unstructured days had worn thin, and that's why Don started a second career in real estate. He works a minimum of six days a week and is first to arrive at the office and often the last to leave. He is a workaholic. When he gets home, he fixes a drink, turns on the TV, and stays glued to the tube the rest of the night. His routine varies only when he and Jessica go out to dinner or when one of their other grown kids is visiting. Then he's more available. Since both he and Jessica changed the subject whenever the conversation turned to their retarded daughter, it was unclear whether or not he spends time with her. It doesn't seem too likely, though, when he's gone most of the day and watches TV in the evenings.

The fact that Don also has process addictions is not surprising. Most married women who are shopping addicts have husbands who have at least one addiction. To clarify that a little further, I made a distinction between hobbies and addictions on the questionnaires that were completed for this book. The first question was, "What are your husband's interests and hobbies?" That question was followed by, "Is your husband addicted to anything such as alcohol, cigarettes, TV, sports, drugs, etc.?" Interestingly, most husbands had very few interests, but many addictions. According to the women, 50 percent of their mates were addicted to TV. The next most common addiction was work, and that was followed by addiction to projects. Only one husband was identified as having a drinking problem. Because my sample was small, the results are only suggestive, not conclusive. Nonetheless, it appears that women with process addictions are often married to men with process addictions, as opposed to chemical addictions. To put it another way, women hooked on shopping are frequently married to men who are hooked on TV and work.

COADDICTED MARRIAGES

When both partners in a marriage have addictions, their relationship is characterized by certain patterns. You can see some of them reflected in Jessica and Don's marriage, and they may be present in your marriage as well. The following list of common relationship patterns is from *In Sickness and in Health*, by Mary S. Stuart.

COMMON PROBLEMS IN CO-ADDICTED RELATIONSHIPS

- Their compulsions center around work, money, and (perhaps) binges.

- Both partners are driven, and they try to avoid their emotional pain.

- Their arguments center around control, working, and spending.

- Both are anxious, depressed at some level, and have shaky self-esteem.

- Both feel that the other's behavior is a reflection on him or herself.

- Both try to control each other.

- Both tend to deny feelings, problems, and their addictions.

- Health problems emerge, especially at the end stages of their addictions.

NOTE: Reprinted with the permission of the publisher, Health Communications, Inc., from *In Sickness and in Health* by Mary Stuart, copyright © 1988.

The Steinbergs

The story of Elana and Steven Steinberg, who also had a coaddictive marriage, comes from a book titled *Death of a "Jewish American Princess"* by Shirley Frondorf. Frondorf was a psychiatric social worker who later became a prosecuting attorney in Arizona. Her background gave her the special credentials needed to write the chilling story of this Arizona couple. In 1981 Steven killed Elana by stabbing her twenty-six times in the middle of the night. Their two young daughters clung together in their bedroom, paralyzed with fear as they listened to their mother's screams for help. At his trial, Steven pleaded not guilty by reason of temporary insanity. What drove him over the edge, according to his attorneys, was his wife's excessive shopping and spending. Not only that, Elana had a shrill voice and called her husband at his work and nagged him. As with many women in rape cases, the *victim's* behavior was on trial instead of the defendant's. Apparently, covert sexism, a brilliant defense, and an inept prosecution converged in this trial, and Steven was found not guilty. After the verdict was read, the jurors hugged the handsome, charming defendant and wished him luck.

An examination into the backgrounds of both the husband and wife is revealing. The Steinbergs were originally from Chicago, where each grew up in a middle-class family. Steven's father died under particularly traumatic circumstances when Steven was twelve. His dad had been ill and decided to stay home from work. He stayed in bed, but felt recovered enough after a few days to have a playful wrestling match on his bed with his son Steven. While they were horsing around, the father gasped, had a massive coronary, and died in Steven's arms. The psychological implication of this death for the boy was enormous. Soon after his father's death, Steven started gambling, a habit that grew into a full-fledged addiction. (Many compulsive gamblers experienced abuse or neglect as children, but others have something occur that is truly unusual and traumatic, such as a brush with death in their early adolescence.) Steve's traumatic experience with his father seems to have been the pivotal factor in his gambling. But no one thought much about it. Gambling was a common activity in his neighborhood, but it *was* a secret that Steve hid from his family, and later from his wife, for many, many years.

As a teenager, Elana was attractive, lively, funny, smart, and sometimes outrageous. Ambitious, with beautiful taste, she and her mother would spend hours shopping for the perfect clothes for Elana's petite figure. When she met Steven in her junior year of high school, she was immediately drawn to his terrific looks, easy charm, and street-wise *chutzpah*. They married in their early twenties, had a couple of babies, and eventually moved to Arizona, where Elana's family had relocated. As Steven's gambling escalated, strange things began happening to the couple. When Elana and the kids were away from the house, a number of alleged burglaries occurred, and many of the couple's valuables were stolen. Insurance covered the losses and the money either paid off gambling debts or was used to place more bets. Steve's first *major* gambling loss occurred on a trip to Las Vegas, the same trip during which Elana's diamond wristwatch mysteriously disappeared. This recurring pattern of supposed robberies also happened wherever Steve worked, including at his father-in-law's successful restaurants in Phoenix.

Steve's gambling bets grew larger and larger, but between his job and successful betting he was able to support his family in fairly lavish style. By now Elana had become aware of her husband's addiction, but she told no one. Highly energetic by nature, she tried to ignore her husband's vice and buried herself in countless social activities. She was also a natural and talented, if unschooled, decorator. Everyone commented about the beautiful and creative things Elana had done with her home. "She had an unerring eye for color and texture," as Frondorf relays the story. Another commented, "That house was just gorgeous inside. I really can't describe it, beautiful furniture, beautiful plants. It was something very special." Even her food offerings were works of art that dazzled her friends. People were also impressed by how immaculate the house was kept. "Sometimes she would get up at three in the morning and clean the oven or something," another friend related. Elana was further described as nervous, hyperactive, and brutally outspoken, but whatever she did, she did very well.

Steven's gambling escalated and money became tight. Elana grew even more nervous and hyper than usual. She couldn't sit still and she lost a great deal of weight. Soon after that, she was murdered by her husband.

At Steven's trial, very little evidence was presented that indicated that Elana was an addicted shopper, although she may have been a shopaholic. She did spend the money her husband made, but she did not run up her credit cards, as the defense implied, thus supposedly *forcing* Steven into a life of crime. That was the crux of the defense's case: Elana was such a shrill, demanding bitch and reckless spendthrift that her husband had to gamble to bring in enough money to satisfy her. Since she never relented in her demands on him, he finally "snapped," and in a moment of temporary insanity, he stabbed his wife to death. The jury chose to believe his version.

Although Elana was a shopaholic, from this therapist's point of view, her obsessive-compulsive disorder was far more troublesome. This point may seem a little confusing, because *addicted shoppers* have the same underlying diagnosis—obsessive-compulsive neurosis. In Elana's case, however, her disorder took another direction—she was fanatical and perfectionistic about her home, she had trouble relaxing and she was a compulsive talker. While a woman with these traits would be difficult to live with, so would Steven, a compulsive gambler, an alleged embezzler, and a reputed womanizer.

Interestingly, on the surface their marriage appeared

to others to be a happy one. Elana's parents were worried about Steven's gambling, and one neighbor felt sorry for Steven because Elana was so demanding, but these were the only cracks in the facade of this apparently happy union. In fact, repression was the operative tactic in the Steinberg family. This was a family that seemed to talk about everything except that which was bothering them. Elana did not badger her husband about his addiction, and whatever rage underlay his brutal murderous act was never expressed to her directly by Steven. After the trial ended and Steven was released from jail, he gave Elana's parents guardianship of his two daughters and then disappeared.

The Steinberg marriage was an extreme example of a codependent marriage. Happily, relationships such as theirs rarely come to such a ghastly end. But when there is addiction in a marriage, one or both marital partners will be in distress. The form that the difficulty takes will depend on the structure of the marriage.

OTHER MARITAL PATTERNS

Mary Stuart believes that people with addictions tend to form seven other predictable relationship patterns. They are:

1. Abuser-victim relationships, in which one party is physically abused. This kind of relationship is most likely found where the husband (or wife) is chemically addicted to alcohol or other non-prescription drugs. Since Steven Steinberg committed the ultimate act of abuse in killing his wife, their marriage could fit into this category. Generally, though, the abuse is an ongoing pattern.

2. Silent type–loudmouth relationships, in which the silent husband is afraid of his emotions and

the talkative wife is afraid of her emptiness. "The more she emotes, the less he listens; and the less he listens, the more emotive she becomes," says Stuart. She goes on to say that in this type of marriage, there is always a great deal of anger operating at an unconscious level. The Steinbergs almost fit into this category, except that Steven was not the reclusive, silent type who had little to say.

3.   Triangular relationships, in which a third person is unconsciously brought between the couple, so that neither has to deal with his or her fears of intimacy or trust. The third person is often a child, whom the parents focus on so that they may avoid their own troubles. This third person also suffers emotionally.

4.   Doctor-patient marriages. I think therapists tend to have this kind of relationship, among others. Accustomed to tending to our clients' mental health, we scrutinize our spouses' moods, moves, and motives for things they may not understand about themselves (this is arrogant, to say the least). Our marriages can be enmeshed (overinvolved) and controlling. Therapists, of course, are not the only ones who fall into this relationship category. Remember Pat from the first chapter—the wealthy woman who hid purchases from both of her husbands? She and her husband Bob have some of these same dynamics operating in their relationship. Pat has had many health problems over the years, and Bob gets as involved in her health care as diligently as he does in his own company. If Pat has scheduled an appointment with a new physician, Bob often will check the person out before Pat's first appointment. He also will ac-

company her to her first visit and even subsequent appointments. He and the physician may have protracted, technical discussions about her problem while Pat merely tunes in.

On the surface this seems like very loving behavior, and it *is* agreeable to both of them. However, according to Robin Norwood, quoted in Stuart's book: "When we do for another what he can do for himself . . . when we prompt, advise, remind or cajole another person who is not a young child . . . this is controlling. Our hope is that if we can control him, then we can control our own feelings where our life touches his." Thus, Bob may be controlling his own fears, or perhaps his frustration, regarding his wife's health.

5. The merger relationship occurs when both partners see each other as life rafts and the two become addicted to each other and their mutual relationship.

6. Distance keepers keep each other at arm's length when both partners are uneasy with intimacy. At the same time, unconscious fears of abandonment keep them together, even if they're getting little out of the marriage.

7. Addict-enabler relationships are those in which the spouse of an addicted person passively allows the other to get away with his or her addiction without confronting the issue. Enabling allows everyone involved with the problem to ignore it or cover it up. Don, for instance, enables Jessica's addicted shopping by not putting pressure on her to seek help. This situation is also typical of many marriages in which one partner is an alcoholic.

If you look over this list and find that you and your husband (or lover) do not necessarily fit into one category or another, that is not unusual. Relationships are so complicated that you may have some aspects of all seven of the patterns listed above, yet not fit squarely into one grouping or another. That's true of Vicki and Phil. Vicki is highly dependent, yet she is most comfortable in a distant relationship. Phil is verbally abusive but would like a closer relationship. Both resort to addictive behavior when under stress, Vicki to shopping and Phil to food (he's at least fifty pounds overweight).

No matter which of the seven categories most marriages fall into, all codependent marriages (marriages in which one or both partners act addictively or compulsively) have the following behaviors and feelings in common:

1. Excessive reliance on denial.

2. Compulsive behaviors or addictions.

3. Poor self-esteem.

4. Confusion about whose feelings are whose. Often one person projects his or her feelings onto the other.

5. Problems with responsibility issues.

6. Problems with intimacy.

7. Depression and anxiety.

8. Stress-related illnesses.

Vicki and Phil

Following are excerpts from two of Vicki's therapy sessions that illustrate some of the codependent behaviors (listed in the previous section) that operate in their marriage (my comments are in parentheses).

Vicki came to her third therapy session puzzled about the fact that she had gone on a shopping bender. She didn't understand why she had done this.

THERAPIST: If you go back in your mind over the past twenty-four hours, you can probably find a connection—something Phil said—that triggered a feeling in you: anger, depression, hurt. Or you may need to go back a little further and see if there's a feeling you repressed a while ago, because repression is often involved in your feelings and subsequent shopping sprees.

VICKI: *(She thought about my comments for a while and then responded indirectly.)* But you can't always just say something! You can't, just because you feel like saying something, always say it. Not if you think about the other person. I can say all I want to myself or to Billy, my dog, who's my buddy. But, if I feel like saying something to Phil, I can't just yell it out at him. He wouldn't understand that. He would get mad, he would get upset, and I, once again, would have ruined his day. He's a great one for telling me I've ruined his day.

THERAPIST: That's how he keeps you from expressing yourself.

VICKI: Oh!

THERAPIST: It's not possible for you to ruin his day.

VICKI: No, that's what I think, what I feel. How can I ruin his day? Why does he rely on me to make his day? Why does he rely on me to make his day a good day or a bad day when he initially starts out in the morning?

What Vicki is identifying here is boundary blurring. This occurs when a mate loses track of where he or she ends and the other person begins. It's as if Phil is connected to Vicki by an emotional feeding tube or umbilical cord. If Vicki says something that upsets Phil, it magically swooshes across the tube that joins them and Phil now feels lousy. Neither of them is aware, yet, that they are responsible only for their own feelings and reactions. One person cannot force another person to feel any particular emotion.

THERAPIST: Yes, that's absurd.

VICKI: If that's what it takes, I can't do it, I can't be this yo-yo.

THERAPIST: And you cannot be responsible for both his feelings and your own.

VICKI: Except that's what I'm asking him to do for me, in a way, I think.

THERAPIST: In what sense?

VICKI: Well, by my spending. I'm saying, "You don't make me happy. You just did something that upset me." I want him to change all these things in him so that I'll be happy.

THERAPIST: I don't know if it's so much to make you happy as it is a wish that he would take your feelings into consideration and stop acting like the gestapo.

VICKI: Oh, and that's not the same thing?

THERAPIST: No, not exactly. You're not saying, "Phil, I haven't anything in my life that enables me to make myself happy, so it's all up to you." You are reacting to Phil's verbal abuse. You *are* holding him accountable for the abuse, which is very appropriate. It is his abusive tongue that puts you down in front of other people. That is his responsibility. What you do about it is your responsibility.

VICKI: Well, last week we had this long talk about how he talks to me and then we went out to dinner with some friends. And when he talked, I could hear the same old thing in his voice—the critical inflection. I tightened up. And so, as soon as we left I said, "Please don't talk to me that way." But he doesn't even know that he does it, so how could he change it?

THERAPIST: Oh, I suspect he knows when he's doing it. He's not stupid.

VICKI: Well, no, he's not stupid.

THERAPIST: And if it is a habit, and he's not necessarily aware of it every time, he is still responsible for what comes out of his mouth. To put it another way, if he were getting this consistent kind of feedback from someone in his business, someone who said that he was not measuring up, he would most likely hear the complaint and try to change his behavior.

VICKI: Yes, I know it. I don't think he talks to anyone else the way he talks to me. He does it to me because he knows I'll put up with it. And I won't make a big stink in public. By the time we're alone, it's too late to make a big stink about it.

THERAPIST: Well, there is a variety of things you can begin doing in these situations. For instance, when you and Phil are out to dinner with friends and he gets abusive, you can quietly excuse yourself from the table and leave.

VICKI: What? What if we're the ones driving. I can't just take the car and leave them all stranded.

THERAPIST: No, that wouldn't be kind. But you could call a cab.

VICKI: But what if we're in San Francisco?

THERAPIST: Cabs go from San Francisco to San Jose.

VICKI: Yes, but that would cost a fortune.

THERAPIST: I think you can afford it.

VICKI: So you're suggesting I just get up right in the middle of dinner and walk out. Just like that?

THERAPIST: Yes. I don't think you would have to do it too often before Phil got the picture that if he is rude to you, you will leave, and he will be the one left feeling embarrassed.

VICKI: I never thought of that. You know, there have been so many times when we've been at antique conventions, and Phil's been nasty, that I've just wanted to just get on the next plane and fly home.

THERAPIST: It's certainly an option to consider. That way you're not stuck, hurt and furious, until the convention's over.

VICKI: Well, don't you think that would be unfair to Phil? If I walk out, just like that?

THERAPIST: No, I don't think it's unfair. I think it's a logical consequence of his behavior. If you decided to do this, though, you might want to inform him of your new plans. That way, he'll be forewarned and can make a more conscious decision about his behavior.

VICKI *(brightening considerably):* I like that, I really do. I never thought about just leaving. God, it would feel so good. Okay, here's another problem. Phil wants new carpet put in his office, and he wants it done by Friday. That's two days from now.

THERAPIST: And if you say to him, "There's no such thing as getting it done in the next two days," what happens?

VICKI: He says, "There's no such thing as *not* getting it done."

THERAPIST: And if you say to him, "Then *you* handle it"?

VICKI: Oh, the fight that would go on if I said, "I don't want to do that; *you* do it." I'd like to say, "I don't want to do it," but I don't do anything else anyway.

Vicki's low self-esteem keeps her from considering asserting herself.

THERAPIST: I don't believe that you don't do *anything* else, but let's say it's true. The point is that you've previously told me you want to get disengaged from his business.

VICKI: Yet, a part of me always wants to know what's happening. I always have to know what's going on in there, because I don't want to be totally ignorant of his business.

THERAPIST: All right, but it sounds as if Phil's setting you up for the impossible. He wants those carpets by Friday, and you can't get them.

VICKI: I know, I know, and I don't know what I'm going to do. It can't be done. He's going to insist anyway.

THERAPIST: And if you say, "I don't wish to do that."

VICKI: I couldn't say it. I wouldn't have the guts to do it.

THERAPIST: Because?

VICKI: He might get upset with me, there's no question he would. Then he'd yell at Ken (the carpet installer).

THERAPIST: That's Ken's problem. Phil and Ken's problem.

VICKI: Right, but that embarrasses me.

This is more indication of boundary problems in the relationship. Vicki's having a hard time separating Phil's behavior toward someone else from her own feelings. For example, if Phil does something embarrassing, she's embarrassed.

THERAPIST: You can decide not to be there. Then you don't have to hear it.

VICKI: Well, all I can say is, I'll try.

THERAPIST: I think the toll on you must be substantial. If you don't get everything done on Phil's lists, you're going to get in trouble. Yet, most of the time you don't really want to be involved in his business. I would think the whole situation would make you both anxious and resentful. And there are definite overtones of a parent-child relationship going on as well.

VICKI: Right. In the old days, Phil thought I was very disorganized, so every morning he'd make me get out pen and paper and make a list of all the things he wanted done.

THERAPIST: Oh God.

VICKI: In those days, I'd kill myself to get the list done. I don't do that now.

THERAPIST: Good.

VICKI: He doesn't usually give me lists anymore, unless he has a lot of stuff he needs done.

THERAPIST: But there seems to be an underlying agreement that you are his gofer.

VICKI: Yes, yes. He says he doesn't give me all this stuff to do just because he doesn't want to do it. It's just that he doesn't have the time to do it himself.

THERAPIST: That may be. I'd like to give you some homework for next week.

VICKI: Do I have to write it down on a list? *(Laughter.)*

THERAPIST: No, but I would like you to think about what role you want to play in your husband's business. Not what he needs, not what you think will make him happy, not what the company needs, but what would make you happy.

VICKI: Okay.

IS YOUR SPOUSE MAKING THINGS DIFFICULT?

In chapters 9 and 10, I'll be discussing relationships at much greater length. But first I'd like to forewarn you about something that occurs in nearly every family when one member is trying to change his or her behavior. It's called sabotage, which sounds very deliberate and sinister but really isn't. Some background first. All families, and even organizations, are unconsciously guided by a goal called "homeostasis," or keeping things the same. People resist change for any number of reasons. First, if a person's behavior remains constant, then he or she is predictable. And when people are predictable, we automatically know how to respond to them and know how they will respond to us. That brings a feeling of security to everyone in the family. Trouble can arise when one person starts changing, because other family members now have to adjust *their* behavior, and they're not sure how to do that. Rather than deal with all of the ambiguities of change, the family members unconsciously try to get things back to the way they were. It's easier and feels safer. They do this by sabotaging the changes another family member is trying to make.

Here's an example from my practice. A client named Laura has been working very hard to kick her shopping addiction, and she's learned from experience that the most important way for her to do so is to stay away from stores, just as a recovering alcoholic may avoid bars.

Laura had ordered an expensive outfit from a local store, then decided that it was too extravagant and she didn't really want it. She could take the dress back herself, but she's learned that all she has to do is step into a store, and she'll find all sorts of things she wants. Rather than expose herself to temptation, she asked her husband to return it for her. He refused, citing how difficult it was to park near the store. Laura thought the excuse was lame and was furious at her husband for not supporting her. After all, he'd been complaining about her shopping for years. When she came in for therapy the following week, we discussed the situation and looked at the fears her husband might harbor about the changes she's making. For instance, many spouses secretly fear that if their husband or wife grows stronger and kicks the addiction, they will leave the marriage. Or, as mentioned in the beginning of the chapter, if the addict relinquishes her addiction, the spotlight may shift to *his* addictions.

If as a couple you've made the unconscious bargain: "I won't nag you about your shopping if you won't get on my case about my watching TV," then your spouse may feel threatened when you change. Consequently, it's realistic to expect mixed messages from your husband as you grapple with your shopping problem. One day he truly will delight in your progress, another he may feel frightened and seem insensitive and nonsupportive. If you find him sabotaging you now and then, try to understand. It's not conscious or deliberate. Rather than making *him* the obstacle to your recovery, take the responsibility for your problem back into your own hands and work around him. When Laura got over being angry at her husband, she was able to think of several ways to get the dress back that didn't involve him. At the end of the session she sat up a bit straighter and said, "After all, it isn't his problem, is it? It's mine, and I'll figure out what to do."

IF YOUR SPOUSE OR LOVER HAS A SHOPPING PROBLEM

Although this chapter is about men who love *women* who shop too much, I think the following anecdote makes it clear that shopping and spending addictions are not limited to women. Men have the problem too. One day an enchanting woman in her late fifties, Iris, came in to discuss her husband's spending problems. She was frantic because he was spending enormous amounts of money almost every day. A recently retired inventor, he had converted their gargantuan basement into a work area, where he continued to tinker with new inventions. His wife didn't mind this at all, but she was upset about his daily trips to the hardware and computer stores, where he spent hundreds of dollars. Whenever they went out to dinner with friends, he always picked up the check, which could also run in the hundreds. Last, he was continually dissatisfied with his fancy cars, so he traded them in every few months.

Although the couple still had a million in the bank, they'd had three million when he retired two years ago. She was panicked that this last nest egg was going to get blown and they'd end up with nothing. Iris is not materialistic, and she really is not as concerned with the possession of money as she is with the waste of it. She also hoped to leave some to her children, but at the rate her husband was spending, there would be little to pass on.

Iris had discussed her fears with her husband, but he pooh-poohed them, saying he was just getting ready to sell another invention and everything would be fine. Because her husband was in the denial phase of his problem, repeated attempts to convince him that he was addicted went unheard. She wanted to know what she could do. The following are suggestions I made to her. Perhaps they will be helpful to you, too, if you spouse is addicted:

What to Do if Your Spouse Is Addicted to Shopping: Fourteen Steps

1. With your spouse's consent, work out an arrangement to set aside three quarters of your savings in a long-term note, so that cash won't be so readily available.

2. Approach your spouse once again with your concerns. I suggest reading *The Language of Love*, by Gary Smalley and John Trent, which offers creative, effective ways to say things to a spouse. (Techniques from that book will be discussed in chapter 9.)

3. Generally, one should approach a spouse with love and care, trying to stay focused on one's own fears rather than the spouse's irresponsible behavior.

4. Ask your spouse to go with you to a counselor to discuss your fears. If he or she is unwilling to go, then go by yourself to get some feedback and support.

5. If allowed, you might also invite your spouse to accompany you to a Debtors Anonymous meeting. Going to the first meeting can be terrifying, but eventually the addict feels enormous relief and camaraderie with others who have the same problem.

6. If your spouse refuses to go, call the local contact person and see if you might be able to go alone. You'll get terrific insight into your spouse's trouble by attending one or more of these meetings.

7. If you cannot attend a Debtors Anonymous group, other options are an Adult Children of Alcoholics or Dysfunctional Families (ACA) group or an Al-Anon group. All offer insight and support to people living in addictive families. From these meetings you will learn about yourself as well as gain tips about how to deal with your addicted spouse.

8. Since your financial safety and security may be in jeopardy, you may want to take steps to

protect certain assets. It is usually best to be above board about this. Also, try to accomplish it in as neutral a way as possible, as opposed to being punitive or parental.

9. Establishing budgets with your spouse rarely works, because this is not a budgeting problem, but rather an addictive one. Nonetheless, sitting down together and setting aside a sum of money for your spouse to spend, no questions asked, may be helpful. That way, he or she will not have to hide purchases, but can share them with you without guilt or remorse. That will help break the anticipation-excitement-pur-chase-high-guilt-depression addictive cycle. If your spouse is willing, ask him or her to share with you his or her struggles and transgressions. (When I feel like I'm warming up for a bender, or if I'm in the middle of one, I almost always talk it over with my husband. He is never out-wardly judgmental or angry; he just let's me think out loud about why I'm doing it or what's really bothering me. He does, of course, get worried or angry when money's tight and I'm not cooperating. But that's helpful to me, be-cause he's holding up the mirror of reality. Sometimes I'm angry or rebellious at first, but eventually the real picture sinks in and I curtail my spending.)

10. This may sound absurd, but discuss with your spouse the possibility that he or she handle all the finances: paying the bills, doing the insur-ance submissions, and so on—all the tedious and sometimes worrisome details of getting things to come out even at the end of the month. (I am much more responsible when it's up to me to get the bills paid. When it's in my

husband's hands, I can con myself easier. We have a deal that I handle the finances except when I'm writing a book. However, when he's through paying the bills each week, we discuss where we stand: what's left in the checking account—or, to be more accurate, how close we are to reaching the limit of our instant credit line. Then we talk about what expenses are coming up, and so on. These discussions keep me informed and dampen my natural tendency to think that everything is rosy.)

12. Try not to nag and harangue your spouse, and don't talk down to him or her. If your spouse is actively working on the problem, then try to hold your tongue. If your spouse isn't doing anything, then periodically bring up your feelings. Don't let your silence support his or her denial.

13. Keep reminding yourself that this is your spouse's problem, and that there's not a lot you can do about it except take care of yourself.

14. Now that this book is available, ask your spouse to read it. Or offer to read it together. However, it's unlikely that he or she will cooperate if denial exists. People who are in denial truly do not believe they have a problem, and even those who know there's a problem are terrified of giving up their addictions. It is nearly impossible for them to picture life without shopping, even if they want to quit.

Addictions are very hard to understand, because quitting seems to be a simple matter of applying logic, self-discipline, or willpower. Unfortunately, quitting requires far more because addictive behavior is caused by both conscious and unconscious *beliefs* and *behaviors*.

This means that behavior cannot change until the underlying problems and beliefs are exposed, addressed, and changed. Such changes take time. For a very few, an addiction can be kicked in a few weeks or months. For the majority, it is more realistic not to expect change for at least three months to a couple of years. Also, it is reasonable to expect backsliding. Almost all change occurs in a zigzag fashion that eventually evens out into a smooth curve upward. So be prepared for a couple of bumpy, but interesting, years as your partner fights his or her addiction. If things go well, both of you will come out wiser and your relationship even stronger.

Part Two

Famous and Not-So-Famous Spenders

Chapter 7

Princess Diana, Jackie, Imelda, and Mary Todd

In February 1986 the world watched to see if a diminutive woman, dressed in a modest yellow outfit, could accomplish the impossible—vanquish the most ruthless and corrupt leader in modern Philippine history. When Corazon Aquino succeeded, we cheered and relished the satisfying pictures of a stooped and disoriented Ferdinand Marcos deplaning in Honolulu. Behind him came his wife, Imelda, impeccably dressed, as always, but apprehensive and lacking her usual hauteur.

Within days, the American government released an inventory of the loot that the Marcoses and their party had brought with them. The diamonds, pearls, and tiaras did not surprise people; such jewels were expected of someone of Imelda's glitzy, world-class stature. Later, however, Filipino officials discovered Imelda's vast closet, which contained, among other things, 65 parasols, 15 mink coats, 508 floor-length gowns, 71 pairs of sunglasses, and 1,060 pairs of size 8½ shoes. Five shelves supported unused Gucci handbags still stuffed with paper, their price tags still attached. Reposing elsewhere were gallon bottles of unopened perfume, vats of Dior wrinkle cream, and hundreds upon hundreds of black bras, panties, and girdles. This discovery was far more shocking than the crates of jewels, because the public could relate to the enormity of such ordinary things as shoes and underwear. What waste, what greed! many people thought. The woman must be sick!

Some women, though, were quietly relieved, because at least *they* didn't have the problem as bad as Imelda did. But millions of women *do* have a shopping problem, and Imelda's outrageously extravagant wardrobe merely reveals how severe the problem can become. Other celebrated women, Princess Diana for instance, are shopaholics who resort to excessive shopping only occasionally, when they are under stress. For numerous others it is the main weapon in their problem-solving arsenal, and they've become addicted. Throughout her two unhappy marriages, which covered much of her adult life, Jackie Kennedy Onassis's addicted shopping was restrained only by the size of her husbands' fortunes. Nor is the shopping addiction limited to this century. Mary Todd Lincoln's son brought a charge of insanity against her because of her lifelong shopping compulsion. Clearly, though, the deposed Filipino despot's wife ranks high on the shopping addiction historical list, for pitiful Imelda strip-mined her country of everything that glittered.

Pitiful Imelda? How is it possible to feel compassion for this hypocritical, greedy, and power-crazed woman? Because she, like the other three famous spenders in this chapter, has suffered greatly—as a child, as an adolescent, and as a wife. The details of these four women's lives differ, but aspects of their personalities bear an uncanny resemblance to one another. As you read about their lives, certain themes will recur: death or divorce of parents, powerlessness as a child, shaming and humiliation, fascination with clothes at a very young age, creativity, denial, repression, perfectionism, and orderliness.

FAMOUS CHRONIC SHOPPERS: FOUR PORTRAITS

Childhood and Adolescence

Princess Diana

Like Jackie, Mary, and Imelda, Diana Spencer saw the cornerstone of her childhood security—her parents' marriage—dissolve before she turned seven. A happy, extroverted, and friendly child until then, Diana nonetheless earned the affectionate nickname "Duch," short for Duchess, ironically, because of her queenlike ways and her fierce stubbornness. She loved parties and party dresses and had a passion for all clothes as a little girl. When her neighbors Prince Edward and Prince Andrew were at their country home, known as Sandringham, Diana was a frequent playmate.

Diana's happy and bucolic childhood changed abruptly when her mother, Frances, fell in love with Peter Shand-Kydd, an attractive, extroverted, funny man who subsequently was divorced by his wife. Diana's father, on the other hand, was quiet and slightly boring and, like his own father, preferred the company of animals to people. Diana's elegant, fun-loving mother was far happier with the more compatible Kydd, and in time she moved from the Spencer's country home to London. Diana and her younger brother went with their mother, while the two older girls remained with their father, thus bringing about a traumatic fracture of the family unit.

The Spencers' eventual divorce grew ugly as they battled for custody of their children. Frances's mother turned against her and sided with Earl Spencer in his quest for custody. Named as an adulteress in the Shand-Kydd divorce, Frances eventually lost custody and the younger children had to return to live with their father. Although he was a loving father, Spencer was inexperienced as a full-time single parent and turned to the nannies for help. Brooking no substitute for their mother, the kids raised hell. They locked the governesses in rooms and on occasion tossed the governesses' clothes out third-floor windows. Rebellion was only the exterior manifestation of the children's misery. Diana regressed and spent long, solitary hours in the nursery dressing her teddy bears in her brother's baby clothes. Shyness replaced extroversion; she no longer looked people in the eye. Her neatness became compulsive and she developed a nervous blush. To protect her from their strife, her parents sent her away to boarding school, and so at nine, a sad, frightened Diana arrived at Riddlesworth Hall with a single suitcase and her pet guinea pig, Peanuts.

Diana spent alternate weekends with her mother and her father and most of her summers at her mother's farms, first in England and later in Scotland. At Riddlesworth and subsequent boarding schools, Diana was well liked by both teachers and peers. Her friends found her fun, thoughtful, and kind, but she was also private, controlled, self-contained. She never discussed her parents' divorce, although her classmates were well aware of the divorce and the charges of adultery brought against her mother. She undoubtedly found the subject painful and embarrassing. In a perverse twist of fate, Diana's father, by now a lord (his father had died), fell in love with a married woman, Raine, who in turn lost custody of her four children to her husband during their divorce because of her adultery with Lord Spencer. This occurred when Diana was fourteen. It seems reasonable to assume that her embarrassment turned to shame with both parents now involved in highly publicized scandals.

Academically, Diana was a disaster. She failed twice to pass her "O levels," exams that allow British students to continue on to what would be considered the eleventh and twelfth grade in this country. Since both of Diana's older sisters had passed these same exams with high marks, it seems doubtful that intelligence was the reason Diana didn't succeed. More likely she was like millions of other teenagers who underachieve when their home lives are in turmoil. By this time Diana was having to cope not only with her parents' divorce, but also with a stepmother she disliked.

Done with school at sixteen, Diana lived with her mother in London for a while, then tried a finishing school in Switzerland, which she detested and left within a few months. Talented and devoted to ballet, Diana longed to become a dancer, but she was unable to do so because of her five-foot-ten-inch height. Adrift and back in London once again, she bought a small flat with an inheritance left to her by her paternal grandfather and went to work as a maid–baby-sitter and later as an assistant at a nursery school.

Jackie Kennedy Onassis

Adultery and divorce left even deeper scars on another little girl who was to become an internationally renowned princess of society, Jacqueline Bouvier. Jackie never even had the seven years of security that formed the core of self-worth that sustains Diana. Her mother, Janet Lee Auchincloss, was tough, ambitious, competitive, and a social climber. When she married Jackie's father, nicknamed "Black Jack," partly for his sensational dark looks, Janet landed not only a handsome man but one with excellent social connections. However, she got more than she had bargained for, because Black Jack Bouvier was also a notorious womanizer who made no attempt to reform after his marriage. Humiliated and unable to control her husband's philandering, Janet flew into uncontrollable rages that digressed from his parade of women to his disappointing income, his horses, his dogs, the children's nurses, and even the children themselves. Jack adored his two beautiful daughters, Lee and Jackie, but his concern and indulgence became yet another source of discontent in his marriage. A cool, aloof, and critical mother, Janet was jealous and resentful of her husband's attachment to their children.

Subjected to her mother's rejection, her father's lavish affection, and her parents' incessant quarreling, Jackie developed into an unhappy, solitary child who frequently drifted off by herself to sketch, write poems, or ride her beloved horses. At school her behavior was unpredictable. She was extremely mischievous and unmanageable, yet such a loner that the other children nicknamed her "Jacqueline Borgia."

Like Princess Diana's parents' divorce, Jackie's parents' divorce was nasty and highly publicized. Janet charged Jack with adultery, and Jackie's private school peers were informed of the scandal by their parents. Jackie withdrew into herself even further, and her Bouvier relatives noticed an embarrassed, sheepish air about her, as if she were deeply ashamed. The divorce didn't end the acrimony between Jackie's parents; her mother was especially vindictive. Jealous of her daughters' love for their father, she did all she could to sabotage his visits with the children and even instructed their nanny to spank the girls if they were caught crying about their absent father. When Jackie's father was able to visit with the girls, he took them on lavish shopping sprees to F.A.O. Schwartz for toys and Saks Fifth Avenue for clothes. As Janet and Jack continued their tug-of-war over their children for the next fourteen years, the battle profoundly affected Jackie's character. She began to crave one thing above all others—respectability and status. Intelligent and gifted, this canny little girl also learned how to play one parent off the other in order to get material things she wanted. Her ability to manipulate people carried over into adulthood.

During her teens, Jackie's relationship with her father deteriorated and became more distant. Worn down by Janet's constant interference and his own strained financial situation, Jack was outraged when Jackie continued charging items on his accounts without his permission. But Jackie did not grow closer to her mother during this period; rather, she became alienated from both parents. Nonetheless, as she matured she used her father as the ideal by which she measured every man, and she was always attracted to older men who reminded her of her dad.

Jackie's aloofness with her peers continued at Vassar, where she was not well liked. Rejected by the elite "Daisy Chain" sorority, Jackie's pride and self-esteem plummeted. It's unclear when she learned to express her hostility through her hilarious, albeit cutting, mimicry of others, but adolescence seems a likely time that a sensitive girl would incorporate whatever means she had to strike back at those who had hurt her.

Imelda Marcos

Imelda Marcos was born the same day and year as Jackie, July 2, 1929. She was the oldest child of her father's second marriage. His first wife, with whom he had had five children, had died. To understand Imelda, it's necessary to understand her father, Vicente Orentes, who was the pampered youngest son in his family. His mother indulged him to the point where he developed little inner strength or self-confidence, and he became chronically dependent on his highly successful older brother, Norberto. So from the outset, Imelda's family was the poor relations of both her uncle's family and the whole Orentes clan.

Imelda's mother, Remedios, was convent-educated, sweet, and docile, with a beautiful singing voice. When she married Imelda's father, she inherited five stepchildren who resented her immediately and tormented her at every opportunity. Imelda's mother made a few feeble pleas to Vicente to keep his children in line, but he did nothing. Like Jack Bouvier, Imelda's father was an irresponsible, carefree, fun-loving man. But Vicente carried his selfishness further. He simply ignored the chaos and near poverty in his household and did whatever he pleased. As more children were born into this miserable family, Imelda's mother grew weaker and more depressed. Disgusted with her husband's neglect, she left Vicente, but always returned. As biographer Carmen Pedrosa concluded, "Her [Imelda's mother's] softness was her undoing. Had she been more forthright and more demanding, she might have just survived her unhappy marriage."

Unable to endure or fight off the torment of her stepchildren, Remedios moved herself and her children into the garage. It had a cement floor and one small window, but a broken-down car blocked any possible light or ventilation from coming into the room. There the family sweltered in the ever-present humidity. Remedios slept on a table, while the children's beds were fashioned from boards supported by milk boxes. Early each morning Imelda, the eldest child, was sent up to the "big house" to ask for her family's food and daily allowance. Often she would be given nothing. Only the generosity of neighbors passing food through the fence saved the family from starvation. A family helper also brought food and, once, a pair of shoes for Imelda, whose shoes had worn out.

When Imelda was nine, her mother literally gave up and died, and the children were turned over to the care of their hateful stepsister, Lourdes. They were, however, allowed to return to their father's filthy "big house."

Imelda says that she remembers nothing of her childhood.

Following the death of his second wife, Vicente moved his family from the outskirts of Manila to Leyte. But even in Leyte financial difficulties kept the family on the move, and the children ended up living in a Quonset hut.

School was a mixed event for Imelda. A mediocre student, she was shunned by smarter students and experienced yet more humiliation when the school posted the names of students whose tuition was in arrears. Her name was often included. At the same time, she was admired for her beautiful voice and was often chosen to sing solos. As she matured, she hid her extreme bitterness about her poverty and concentrated on using her evolving beauty and lovely voice to bring her recognition. In time she became the town beauty and official hostess, but she confided to a close friend that security would be the most important factor when she chose a husband. In her late teens she moved in with her wealthy and socially prominent cousins in Manila, who treated her like a pet servant. Humiliated but determined to better herself, she docilely endured her relatives' patronizing behabior and plotted her future. She entered beauty contests and eventually became Miss Manila, but that was not enough to admit her into Manila's tightly knit upper-class society.

An uncle commented on her ambition: "When I looked at Imelda, I thought what she really needed was to be loved and protected. But the sort of ambition she had was serious— it should have been only for men, tough men."

Mary Todd Lincoln

When Mary Ann Todd lost her mother at age six, that was just one of a succession of losses that began when she was four and that continued throughout her life. Unlike Imelda, Mary and her brothers and sisters were the children of a prosperous father's first marriage. Born in Lexington, Kentucky, Mary's first loss occurred when her baby brother died. Then her mother gave birth to a daughter, and Mary's father, Robert, wanted to name the baby after his childless sister, Ann. Mary was thus forced to relinquish the Ann in her name and, henceforth, be called Mary Todd. She also gave up her place as youngest child to this younger sister, whom she would always resent. Mary's mother was a placid, cheerful woman, and when she died giving birth to her sixth child, Mary was devastated.

Her emotional, high-strung, successful father was unable to offer much comfort to his young children and instead buried himself in his work. He did find time, however, to meet a woman named Betsey, whom he married with unseemly dispatch. Scandalized and angry, Mary's maternal grandmother resented Robert's new wife, which only inflamed her grandchildren's natural suspicion of their new stepmother. However, Betsey had little time to focus on family infighting, as she produced eight more children in the next eight years.

One of the first overt conflicts Mary had with her stepmother was over clothes. Mary, like Diana and Jackie, had an inordinate fascination with clothes and was enchanted with bouffant summer dresses that puffed and swayed on hoop-skirted ladies. Mary wanted a hoop for her skirts. Her stepmother said she was too young (she was nine), so Mary secretly whipped one up by tying twigs and sticks together. When Betsey saw Mary's homemade contraption, she ordered her to take it off, and then proceeded to bring up the incident so many times in front of others that it became a standing joke in the family. Betsey Todd often used shaming as a way of punishing her children and stepchildren. One of Mary Todd's biographers, Jean Baker, explains the important distinction between guilt and shame: "To be shamed and humiliated is to feel a disgrace to the whole self, not just as with feelings of guilt, where a person understands that a particular transgression has occurred. If the effect of guilt is anxiety, then that of shame is a diminished psyche, *given to quick, defensive anger*." (Italics added.) As we shall see, Mary developed a quick and ferocious temper.

In order to garner attention from her distracted father, Mary used her insightful mind to engage him in political discussions whenever she could snag him long enough to talk. Distant from her stepmother, the only consistent attention Mary received was from her longtime nurse, Mammy, and her maternal grandmother.

Like Jackie Onassis, Mary was not popular at school, but she was respected for her sharp intellect and retentive mind. Often a participant in school plays, she learned through acting how to mimic people. As with Jackie, this mimicry was an unbecoming but funny trait that she polished over the years. Her interest in politics came about in part because of the location of her home in Lexington, Kentucky. An impressive house on a beautiful tree-lined avenue, it was situated only three blocks from the slave prison, where slaves, tied to hickory stakes in the front of the prison, were frequently beaten. While Mary's father had slaves, he treated them with kindness, and Mary was very close to her beloved Mammy. Thus, from birth Mary was brought up to regard all people with decency and compassion. But the geographical location of her family home in Kentucky, a slave state, would become far more important than her beliefs when she became first lady.

At age twelve it was customary for girls to finish school and then turn their attentions to the interlocking concerns of procuring beautiful dresses and landing husbands. Not so for Mary. She wanted more education, and so she continued studying until she was seventeen, living on campus in Lexington, which suited both her and her stepmother. After graduation she was determined to stay out of her father's house. She followed two of her older sisters to Springfield, Illinois, where she stayed for about two years. She was forced to return home when her sisters no longer had room for her in their cramped homes. Back in Lexington, she became a teacher's apprentice at the same school she had attended, and then returned once more to Springfield.

MARRIAGES

The Lincolns

The marriage between Abraham and Mary Todd Lincoln was volatile. But given the differences in their personalities as well as their numerous losses, the Lincolns successfully maintained a genuine love for one another. Abraham's long, sorrowful face was the mirror of his inner state of mind, which was chronically depressed and pessimistic. Mary's shaky self-esteem and traumatic childhood left her vulnerable in several areas. She was extraordinarily sensitive to criticism; she had migraine headaches that would flatten her for days; the deaths of her children threw her into prolonged depressions; and during middle age it appears that she had a hellish time with menopause. Nonetheless, she was witty and usually upbeat, the perfect counterpoint to Lincoln's melancholy personality.

The Lincolns met, married, and settled in Springfield, Illinois, where Abraham practiced law. Their courtship was stormy. Scattered, preoccupied, and forgetful, Abraham lost Mary for a while after he was late picking her up one night for a party. In a huff, Mary went to the party on her own and flirted like mad with all of the available men. When Abraham showed up at the party, Mary ignored him, and their romance faltered. Calling this first quarrel "the fatal first," Abraham became so depressed that friends removed his razor and other means of self-destruction from his room. Mary wasn't happy, either, but their breakup gave her some breathing room. She wasn't quite ready to give up the specialness of being a Todd or the uniqueness of being an educated woman living away from her parents.

After a few months the young couple patched things up, married, and set up housekeeping in a boardinghouse, where they had one small room and a shared parlor. Mary got pregnant almost immediately, and three days short of nine months, the Lincoln's first son, Robert, was born. This was not a particularly happy time for Mary, since Abe was away for about half of the year, riding the law circuit. Because of her childhood losses, Mary perceived any kind of absence as abandonment, and she consoled herself at local department stores, where she purchased and returned clothing with regularity. Her first requirement was that her dresses be outstanding and different—no run-of-the mill calico for her. Often she'd purchase fabric, then decide that it wasn't quite the right shade of color, and send it off to Saint Louis to be redyed to her specifications. Once the material was returned it went to the dressmaker, and after several fittings, the final touches were added—flounces, bows, and, last, the ribbons that became her trademark.

It was the custom to extend credit for prolonged periods of time, so a bill for a given item might not appear for a year. This was not a helpful practice for an addicted shopper like Mary. She learned to be conveniently vague about bills, and began her lifelong habit of buying to make restitution for personal and political defeats.

Mary's father gave the Lincolns money annually, which enabled them to buy their first house. Mary hired household help not so much for their labor as for their company. It was not unusual for her to have the help, her children, or even a male neighbor sleep with her to stave off loneliness when

Abraham was gone. Mary's invitations were not considered scandalous because many lonely men and women slept together simply for comfort, not sex. Despite the rigid Victorian standards of the day, Mary was, nonetheless, a lusty woman, and the Lincoln's terrific sex life helped bridge their many differences. Their letters to one another sizzle with thinly disguised sexual longing.

During the eighteen years the Lincolns spent in Springfield, they had three more sons. After Robert came Eddie, Mary's favorite child, who died of consumption, or TB. Three weeks after Eddie's death, she was pregnant for the third time. This child, Willie, she nursed for eighteen months. Predictably, as soon as she stopped breast-feeding, she became pregnant one more time, this time with Theodore, who was nicknamed Tad. An excellent mother, Mary busied herself not only with her children but also with her husband and his political career. Politics served several purposes: it was an interest Mary enthusiastically shared with Abraham; it brought her publicity and attention, which she craved, and it satisfied her need for drama. Because of her sensitivity and insecurity, Mary was a master at taking offense, yet she relished the ever-changing panorama of her friends and enemies.

After many years of struggle, Mary entered the White House in 1861 ever on the defensive, with a whole agenda of wrongs to right. She was determined to show snobby Washington socialites that she was not a country bumpkin just because she came from Illinois, then considered part of the West. Accomplishing that, of course, required a sensational wardrobe. Like Jackie a hundred years later, Mary meticulously planned her wardrobe. She, too, had a fetish for gloves; she ordered eighty-four pairs just before she moved into the White House. Once in residence, her attention shifted from her temporarily complete wardrobe to the despicable condition of the White House. Again, like Jackie, Mary went on a prolonged spending spree to fix it up. Neither unseasonable weather nor the endless carnage of the Civil War sidetracked

Mary from her many trips to New York and Philadelphia in search of the finest fabrics, furniture, and French wallpapers.

Blatantly ignoring the inadequate budget set aside by Congress for White House upkeep, Mary simply ordered what she wanted and coped with the bills later. Such behavior resulted in many gentle lectures from Abraham, which led to temporary repentance followed by renewed spending.

When it came to her gowns, Mary (like Nancy Reagan) was a little muddled regarding which were gifts to her from her designers and which ones she would be charged for later. Rather than get this delicate issue clarified, Mary simply adopted a most creative rationalization. If, per chance, a tradesman or designer was going to bill her for a purchase, Mary figured that he would likely postpone sending the hated bill as long as she kept buying from him. So she just kept charging. Later, things got trickier. She began doing political favors in exchange for money; there is some evidence that Mary sold a few of her husband's private and highly secret papers to pay off her debts. Her biographers reach different conclusions on this issue, some saying she sold the papers, others saying they were stolen.

During the White House years, Mary spent many happy hours with her three children. Even her most severe critics praised her mothering. Responding to the praise, she said the children helped fill her chronic emptiness and kept her from being alone, which she hated. She was especially attentive to Tad, the youngest, who was hyperactive and a poor student with a speech impediment. Both of the Lincolns were permissive with their boys, and many who visited the White House found the kids obnoxious rather than the little darlings of their parent's eyes. They also encountered the Lincolns' menagerie, which included turkeys, goats, ponies, and cats.

During their White House years, the Lincolns lost still another son, Willie, to typhoid fever at age twelve. Both parents were prostrate with grief. Mary stayed in bed for weeks, while Abraham carried on with his job but spent part of every Thursday (the day Willie died) in the boy's room.

When Abraham was assassinated, Mary was again understandably inconsolable, and it took her many months just to rouse herself sufficiently to move out of the White House, much to the annoyance of President Andrew Johnson and his wife. Returning to Springfield was out of the question. There were too many painful memories there. Eventually she landed in Chicago. Unprotected by the imperial trappings of the presidency, she now had to face her creditors, and over a number of years she paid off ten thousand dollars in debts.

After her stay in Chicago, Mary was emotionally restless and moved frequently, spending many years in Europe, with Tad at her side. By now her oldest son Robert had married and was living in Chicago. On one of their return visits to the United States, Tad became ill and, at age eighteen, died of pleurisy. Bereft again, Mary briefly returned to her old standby—shopping. On one expedition she bought ten pairs of identical lace curtains, even though she lived in a one-bedroom apartment in Chicago (they were for a cottage she planned to buy in Wisconsin, but her son Robert didn't know about this). Mary had been living very frugally since Abraham died, never spending more than her widow's pension and the interest from her husband's estate. But when Mary appeared to be spending recklessly again, Robert decided to protect his eventual inheritance by having his mother proclaimed insane.

Mary's 1875 trial for insanity was chilling. The afternoon she returned from buying the infamous curtains, an attorney and two policeman knocked on the door of her apartment, telling her she was to come immediately and stand trial for insanity. Dumbfounded, she obliged and accompanied them to court, where her son Robert had lined up fifteen witnesses to testify to her instability. Her attorney was essentially chosen by the prosecution, and he did nothing to defend her. Nor was she allowed to say anything in her defense. In short order, the all-male jurors found her guilty of insanity, and she was taken to an institution for the insane on the outskirts of Chicago.

Devastated by her son's betrayal but ever intelligent, Mary

was a model patient, and in three months' time she was released. Humiliated—and terrified of her son—she fled once again to Europe, where she stayed until ill health forced her to return to the United States. She settled with her older sister in Springfield. Prudent with money, and fascinated by it in her old age, Mary invested wisely. Upon her death, she left Robert and his daughter a hefty sum. It's unclear why she included Robert in her will. Perhaps the mother in her was able to forgive her son's betrayal.

The Marcoses

The young Imelda had a chance at a happy marriage, but, predictably, it was sabotaged by her family. At age twenty-three she met a warm, caring man, Ariston, who was in the middle of having his brief marriage annulled. When her rigidly Catholic relatives objected to his previous marriage, Imelda capitulated, and her longing for love and security drifted just out of reach.

Into the breach came Ferdinand Marcos, a ruthless and obsessively ambitious man who, like Imelda, was determined to penetrate the iron gates of Manila society. Although attracted to each other, Imelda and Ferdinand entered their marriage with cold calculation. The centerpiece was their shared determination for power and acceptance. Marriage to the wealthy Marcos also ensured an end to poverty, and Imelda looked forward to the security she desperately needed.

Politically and socially ambitious, Marcos used his extravagant wedding ceremony to accent his debut as a presidential contender. Marriage to the glamorous Imelda, with her highly placed relatives, gave Ferdinand an entrée into the Philippine aristocracy, which otherwise would have eluded him. Marcos no doubt realized that Imelda's beauty would also function as an enormous political asset. However, the marriage soon felt anything but advantageous to Imelda. The ethics and values by which she was raised—meekness, humility, and resignation—were soon subsumed by the wealth and corruption of

Ferdinand's household. For instance, she learned that Ferdinand's cook was paid far more than she had made as a bank clerk. Astounded, Imelda asked Ferdinand if *she* could do the cooking and be paid the cook's salary. Amused, Ferdinand agreed. But the experiment backfired, with results that would eventually affect every Filipino; Imelda discovered that her husband doled out bribes far larger than her cooking salary to each of his cronies every month. Enraged, appalled, and rebellious, Imelda shed her naïveté about her husband's character (and wealth) and never again felt guilty about money or what it could buy. Shortly thereafter, rumors about the spendthrift Mrs. Marcos wound their way through the political grapevine.

But Imelda's newfound financial security and extravagance did not bring acceptance, either by her husband or by society. Upper-crust socialites rejected Imelda because she was not one of them; she did not grow up in their circle or attend the same schools, and her parents were not acquainted with theirs. Painfully insecure when invited to their functions, she made the fatal and embarrassing mistakes of gushing and fawning. At the same time Ferdinand was relentless in his attempts to push her to be what she wasn't—sophisticated, well read, cultured. As the pressure grew, she developed migraine headaches that lasted for days, and eventually she had a nervous breakdown. She was treated in a psychiatric clinic in New York and returned confident and determined "to try new things." Unfortunately, she emerged from her therapy not determined to be herself—ambitious, yes, but a fairly simple and caring woman—but ready to accede to her husband's wishes that she become someone different.

Imelda also discarded her childhood when she traded in her old personality, although repression could not erase her scars. Instead, in what is technically called "reaction formation," she grew to loathe the helpless poor, who unconsciously reminded her of her deepest fear—poverty. Had she not repressed the terrible years of her childhood, she could have used her memories to help her impoverished countrymen rather than rob them, and she wouldn't have needed to spend insatiably to fill the endless well of her terror.

Imelda's shattered perceptions of her husband didn't end when she learned of his corruption. Soon it became clear that he had other women, and despite Imelda's unhappiness, he was not about to give them up. Crushed, she dealt with this blow as she had with others, by shopping. Later, during his presidency, Imelda caught Ferdinand in an especially tacky and publically embarrassing affair, and she used this unsavory situation as leverage to gain power over him. They ultimately arrived at an arrangement that would allow each to do as he or she wished.

After martial law was declared in the Philippines in 1972, the Marcoses had unhampered access to their country's treasury, and they dipped their hands in with abandon. Before martial law, Imelda's personal wealth was about $250 million; by the end of their rule in 1985 it was estimated to be $1.6 billion. Her wealth and position as first lady also offered Imelda unlimited opportunities to travel. She took off whenever she could, whether to Paris or to her townhouse in Manhattan. Two hundred suitcases accompanied her on such short jaunts and for official visits, eight hundred.

Constantly searching for acceptance among white, Western society, Imelda conceived of the idea of an international film festival to be held in Manila. She was determined to impress her jet-set friends with the beauty of the capital city, so she went on a building binge—like Potemkin under Catherine the Great, erecting one lavish but useless building after another. The Filipino press dubbed this her "edifice complex," and to her chagrin, the film festival never took place. Another time Imelda became obsessed with the idea of marrying off one of her daughters to Prince Charles. When that scheme failed, she consoled herself by buying building after building in New York. Finally she turned her obsession for acceptance to the international cafe society, to the jet-setters. There she was more successful and, over the years, developed an international cadre of dilettante friends, including George Hamilton, Christina Ford, and others. While these friendships were exciting, they never appeased the needy inner child that remained within Imelda. History now comes full circle, as the humiliated and exiled former first lady of the Philippines lives as a virtual house prisoner in Honolulu, a woman facing the legal ramifications of her years of excessive shopping and looting while she desperately looks for a new home and a country where she can find asylum.

The Kennedys

By the time the Kennedys reached the White House in 1961, they, too, had an arrangement of sorts. This solution did not come easily, and the early years of their marriage were emotionally tempestuous as Jackie became aware of her husband's compulsive womanizing. Her reactions ranged from glacial silence toward Jack to revenge-motivated shopping raids in Georgetown, as compulsive in nature as her husband's chronic philandering.

The couple met when Jackie was twenty-two and Jack was thirty-five and had just been elected to the Senate. He loved his bachelor life, but political expediency dictated that he, like Marcos, marry and marry well. He could not very well tote along a movie star to the White House. Jackie fit the bill, for she was no Marilyn Monroe. Beautiful, educated, and cultured, with impeccable social credentials, she would also camouflage some of the odor of the Kennedys' bootlegged fortune. Jack offered Jackie much that she needed: an "older man to take care of her" (as she had been brought up to believe was a necessity by her mother) and, ironically, one who would get her out from under her constantly critical mother. Besides, Jack was handsome, powerful, and extremely wealthy. Love did not seem to be an overriding requirement to either of them, although they did love each other in their similarly limited way. Neither had any experience with intimacy, except sexually, and neither was very good at expressing feelings.

None of this was apparent at their much-publicized wedding in 1953. The only odd note occurred when Jackie was escorted down the aisle by her stepfather, Hugh Auchincloss, rather than her father. Jackie's mother's thirst for revenge had never abated, and it was she who called the shots at the wedding. Jackie's father was in Newport, new tux in hand, when Janet systematically began excluding him from the pre-nuptial festivities. By the day of the wedding, "Black Jack," nervous and slightly drunk, waited at his hotel to hear whether or not he would be allowed to walk his daughter down the aisle. He would not. Heartbroken, he left town and saw no part of his beloved daughter's wedding.

When the Kennedys settled in their first home in George-town, Jackie detested the constant comings and goings of her husband's political cronies in *her* home. Solitary by nature, she would retreat upstairs, spending hours reading or super-vising her endless redecorating projects. Further upset by the demands of her husband's political career and his ever-intru-sive family, Jackie progressively became more depressed. Al-though outwardly social, she could tolerate seeing people only every few months, and found self-disclosure impossible, if not repugnant. Interviews with her friends through the early 1970s painted a uniform picture of a remote, deeply unhappy woman who never had healed from her parent's internecine warfare.

Her vulnerability is vividly portrayed by a scene that took place the day of JFK's presidential inauguration. During the parade, all of the Auchincloss, Kennedy, Lee, and Bouvier relatives were invited into the White House for a family gathering. Jack remained outside watching the parade while Jackie went inside, ostensibly to entertain the families. Jackie had not seen many of these family members since her wed-ding, where the humiliating situation with her father had taken place. Her guests waited and waited for her to appear, while she remained upstairs, paralyzed with fear and highly agitated. In despair, she kept repeating to her cousin, Michael Bouvier, "I don't care [if they are expecting me], I can't make it, I just can't." And she didn't. Later, Jack came in and saved the situation. This was just one scene in the ongoing deception of Camelot.

According to one of her aides, Jackie lived a "strangely remote" life in the White House, busying herself with entertainment, her own little family, and projects of her choice. If she did not want to participate in an activity, nothing could drive her to it. She was unable to say no to people directly, however, and left that task to her press secretary. She was equally indirect and secretive about things she wanted. A compulsive shopper, Jackie learned to cloak the whole issue of her purchases in secrecy.

She selected Oleg Cassini as her official wardrobe designer, and he was given the job with the clear understanding that he would not divulge the cost or number of gowns she ordered. In a recent autobiography, however, Cassini broke his silence and said he had made around one hundred dresses for Jackie during the first year of the Kennedy administration and a total of three hundred, which means that Jackie had a new outfit from Cassini about every third day.

Jack's father Joe picked up her Cassini bill, so the Kennedys were never burdened by his charges. But there were other bills—gloves, for instance. Jackie ordered hundreds of pairs from Cassini, and that bill, along with others that Jack Kennedy paid in 1961, totaled $40,000, the equivalent of about $122,000 in 1988. In 1962 she spent $121,000—the president's entire salary—on family expenses alone.

Alternatively worried and enraged, Jack would rail at Jackie about her spending and she would promise to do better. Then she would sit down with her personal secretary and sincerely ask where she seemed to be spending the most. Invariably, her secretary, Mary Gallagher, would reply, "clothing," but Jackie would appear not to hear her and begin scrutinizing budget items like liquor or entertainment. This exercise was repeated many times, with similar results. Jackie would cut back on her spending for a brief period and then plunge in again. In addition to Cassini's creations, Jackie had clothing "scouts" who perused other collections and ordered

things for her that they thought she would like. She compulsively scanned the papers for things she wanted and would
have her secretary order them using a fictitious name.

Both of the Kennedys were given fictitious names by Dr.
Max Jacobson, who regularly made trips to the White House
from his New York office to inject the Kennedys with amphet-
amines, which were not illegal at that time. This startling
revelation comes from two sources—Jacobson's autobiography and C. David Heymann's 1989 biography *A Woman
Named Jackie*. It appears that both of the Kennedys used the
drug to increase their stamina. Jackie also used it to help
relieve the pain of the migraine headaches she suffered. It also
helped her muster the energy she needed to renovate the
White House.

Her observant and creative eye would fall, like Mary Todd
Lincoln's, upon room after room in her private homes as well
as in the White House, and soon each room was stripped and
redone to her tastes. But her taste unfortunately changed with
alarming rapidity, especially after traveling abroad, where she
would pick up new ideas. After Jackie returned home, the
carpenters, painters, paper hangers, and decorators would be
summoned, only to redo a just-finished room. Jackie's perfectionism helped to keep her busy; consequently, no detail was
too small to escape her notice. At one point she became
obsessed with the whereabouts of ash tray plates that were
scattered around the White House, and instructed the curator
of the White House to make sure that each one remained
where she had placed them.

When her husband was assassinated in 1963, Jackie was
truly bereft. Although not close, the Kennedys had reached a
tenuous peace with each other, and Jackie had grown very
dependent on her husband. Her depression after his death
lasted for many months, and it was not until she moved to
New York that she began to recover. However, her stability
was shattered when her brother-in-law Bobby Kennedy was
assassinated in 1968. Once again she sank into a depression,
and she grew deeply concerned for her children's safety.

Thus, her astonishing marriage to Aristotle Onassis begins to make sense when the illusionary Jackie is stripped away and one sees the frightened child-woman who could count on neither safety for the people she loved, nor security or happiness within herself. Her unconscious solution remained unchanged: marry an older man who not only would re-create the sense of love and safety she thought she had had with her father but also support the spending addiction that momentarily filled her inner emptiness. Even her choice of clothing on the day she married (a dress that looked like an adult version of a little girl's party dress, complete with a bow streaming down her shoulder-length hair) supports the picture of the little girl marrying Daddy—or even, God forbid, Grandpa.

As she sadly learned, adult bandages do not heal childhood wounds, and Jackie found only momentary happiness with Aristotle. As the marriage deteriorated, her emotional fix, shopping, escalated to herculean proportions, and she was clocked spending at the phenomenal rate of three thousand dollars a minute. Aristotle's death and the money she ultimately wrested from his estate extricated her from two demons: her unhappy marriage and her nagging insecurity about money.

Between psychoanalysis five times a week and a job that has brought her both self-esteem and a legitimate outlet for her substantial creative gifts, it appears that Jackie no longer uses shopping as much to fill her emptiness. Once again, her favorite male companion is an older-looking man, Maurice Tempelsman, a man estranged from his wife, someone who is wealthy and witty—an altogether safe man who probably will not ask more of Jackie than she can give.

The Prince and Princess of Wales

Prince Charles, like Jack Kennedy, was loathe to give up his bachelorhood, but for different reasons. While both enjoyed affairs with women, Charles lacked the voracious sexual appetite of Kennedy. It was not sexual freedom that Charles feared losing, but the luxury of solitude. Encumbered by the demands of his royal birth, Charles had spent his entire life in the company of regiments of people, from family to servants, doing "the proper thing." The chance to be alone and to be himself had to be more than a simple desire; it probably had become a survival mechanism.

Charles and Diana were reintroduced as adults when Charles was on the rebound from a serious love affair. He was also under severe pressure to find a wife, marry, and reproduce, to ensure the continuation of the monarchy. Besides his initial sexual attraction to Diana, Charles found that she fit his comprehensive requirements for a wife and queen. She had looks, background, temperament, liveliness, affection, and, most important, she was a virgin. In a rather detached way, he proposed. She eagerly accepted, and the romance of the century blossomed. The chaste Diana was said to have moved in with the Queen Mother to learn "queening," but in fact, she moved into a suite of rooms right next to Charles's in Buckingham Palace.

Since Charles was often absent, Diana first tried to quell her boredom by exploring the palace. She was often found down in the kitchen fixing snacks or talking with the staff. But that was hardly stimulating enough for a young, energetic women who was used to work and a busy social life. It was at this point that she started shopping. Distressed with her rather girlish style, she asked her sister to introduce her to the top people at *Vogue,* who set to work helping Diana discover her own, more sophisticated look.

But it was only after their marriage that Charles is said to have really fallen in love with his exuberant and sexy wife. His enthusiasm lasted through the birth of their first child, William, but had decidedly cooled by the time their second son, Harry, was born. After the birth of her first baby, Diana experienced a severe postpartum depression and lost a great deal of weight. At the time, two psychiatrists commented on her depression. One of them was Dr. Thomas Holmes, who, using the Holmes and Rache life stress scale (see chapter 3), tabulated 407 points for Diana, which meant that she stood an 80 percent chance of developing an illness. He thought an obsessive-compulsive illness was likely, which is the underlying disorder in addiction.

The demands of never making a misstep, verbal or otherwise, weighed heavily on Diana, and she felt she wasn't allowed to say anything or do anything but smile and look pretty. Her freedom was gone, her personality engulfed. She began expressing herself in the only way available—through clothes. Although Diana had always loved dressing up, her fascination with clothes turned into a way of life, one that, Diana now recognizes, had become consuming.

As her husband's ardor cooled, shopping also became a way for Diana to attract his attention, although this seems to have been largely unsuccessful. The couple has little in common, except, as one biographer put it, "the shared love of their children and their inability to communicate." Although not without humor, Charles is serious, introspective, intellectual, and bookish. He also adores horses, polo, and hunting, and he is attracted to people who share his interests. Diana, by contrast, is extroverted, and she loves to dance and party, play tennis, read light novels, and attend the ballet. Both find each other's interests and friends boring. Consequently, like the Kennedys and the Marcoses, they have reached an agreement that allows each to pursue his or her own interests. That could be a healthy decision for their marriage, if both are at peace with their differences and simply enjoy each other for the limited activities and interests they do share. It seems, however, that their agreement has resulted in distance rather than a healthy respect for each other's individuality.

Although Diana does have an enormous wardrobe and maintains her love of shopping, she has weathered her emotional and developmental challenges, and has grown into a superb mother and a self-assured woman. She likes herself enough to have clung fiercely to her identity, and she has sufficient mental health and balance to respond to the problems in her life by using a number of coping mechanisms. She no longer turns solely to shopping when she's unhappy.

COMMON TIES

Three of the women in this chapter have been first ladies of their countries, and one will someday be queen, but these women share far more than their exalted status. The secure home life of each was imperiled by either divorce or death when each was between the ages of six and nine: Mary Todd Lincoln and Imelda Marcos experienced the death of their docile and loving mothers and then endured venomous step-family situations. Mary was mistreated by her stepmother and Imelda by her stepsiblings. Jackie's and Diana's parents had traumatic divorces in which embarrassing charges of adultery were hurled against beloved parents. But long before the dissolution of these marriages, Diana, Jackie, and Imelda witnessed their parents' unsettling arguments.

Each of these women experienced humiliation and shame that visibly changed their personalities as little girls. The normally elusive Jackie withdrew into herself still further as she coped with contradictory messages of low self-worth from her mother and entitlement from her father. Formerly extro-verted and cooperative, Diana became shy and naughty, while Mary Todd Lincoln turned feisty and then defensive. Imelda's childhood was riddled with shame and humiliation, an expe-rience so severe that she has repressed almost all of her memories of that time. That repression eventually deadened her conscience to the point that she ravaged the lives of her countrymen. She literally did to her people what had been done unto her. Both Imelda and Mary probably felt a multi-tude of feelings when their mothers died: the horror of abandonment, guilt-engendering anger at their mothers for leaving them, and unexpressed rage at their fathers for leaving them unprotected. Too poor to experience the luxury of pretty party dresses and beloved pets, it's unlikely that Imelda shared the same fascination and comfort with them as Diana, Jackie, and Mary Todd.

Many children who experience the terror of unpredictability and powerlessness crave security, control, and power when they become adults. This was true of Diana, Jackie, Imelda, and Mary Todd. Whether consciously or unconsciously, each woman married politically ambitious and powerful men who they believed might bring them both love and emotional safety. This was not to be. The most devoted and loving husband of the lot, Abraham Lincoln, was nonetheless away on business half of his married life, and he could not protect Mary from the devastating deaths of three of their four sons. Prince Charles certainly has brought Diana riches and the children she adores, but he seems to have checked out emotionally when faced with their incompatibility. Jack Kennedy and Ferdinand Marcos each lacked the will and inclination to give their wives more than cursory attention. Rather, they wreaked havoc with their single-minded political ambition and compulsive unfaithfulness.

Each woman responded with depressions ranging from mild to severe. After the birth of her first child, Diana experienced a severe depression that was brought on not by her husband but by the burden of her position as the most publicized woman in the world. Mary Todd and Jackie went into agonizing depressions that lasted for months following the deaths of their children and husbands. Imelda had a nervous breakdown requiring hospitalization early in her marriage. Mary Todd, Imelda, and Jackie all suffered from migraine headaches that most likely were brought on by the twin pressures of life-styles they could not endure and the anger they felt toward husbands who they felt had abandoned them emotionally.

Of course, disappointing marriages are rarely the fault of one person, and each of these beautifully dressed and spectacular women brought highly sensitive personalities to their marriages. The queen of England once compared Diana to a thoroughbred racehorse: beautiful, high strung, nervy, and in need of settling down. This description could fit the other women as well. Insecure and anxious from unstable childhoods, they share other not-so-enchanting characteristics. All four are perfectionists and have been known to drive those around them to distraction with their obsession with detail. None have been very successful at expressing disappointment and anger in constructive ways. Both Mary Todd and Jackie mimicked those with whom they were angry in humorous but unbecoming ways. Jackie, like Diana, also avoids people when she's angry with them rather than face the discomfort of an open confrontation. Mary Todd was known to some as the "she cat" because of her uncontrollable rages. And, of course, each spent prodigious amounts of money on clothes, furniture, art, and houses to bolster their insecurity, revenge their husbands' neglect, and fill their psychic emptiness. In time Mary Todd, Jackie, and Diana all found healthier ways to deal with their unhappiness, but it seems unlikely that the barefoot child from Manila will ever find peace.

Chapter 8

How I Got Hooked and Unhooked

Solving a problem demands a lot from us: thought, analysis, digging around in our pasts, getting to know ourselves, and figuring out what we need to feel happier. It also takes a bit of time. Answers to my shopping problem came through reading, talking to my own therapist, and taking the time to get to know myself. Even though I was forty-five when I started this process (old enough, I thought, to know myself), I was surprised to discover two things. First, I had been squelching many of my feelings for years, and second, I had changed. A metamorphosis had taken place, but I hadn't noticed it enough to label it or see its significance.

I'm going to start my story in the middle—the time, several years ago, when I realized I had a shopping problem. At that point I had been researching this book for about a year, had taken the tests in chapter 3, and had heaved a sigh of relief when my scores indicated I wasn't addicted. Nonetheless, I knew that something was amiss.

SIGNS OF TROUBLE

I knew I had a problem when:

- *I felt guilty* about the whole subject of shopping.

- *I felt guilty* when I drove into my cul-de-sac with a plastic dress bag flapping away on the backseat hook. If a neighbor was outside, I was sure she thought, My God, she's bought something more!

- *I felt guilty* when my twenty-four-year-old daughter Roz came over for a visit. We'd talk a while, and then first thing I knew, she'd be casually flipping through my closets.
  "What's this?" she'd ask, her voice a mixture of appreciation, envy, and disgust.
  "Oh, *that*. Nothing. Just this little dress (blouse, sweater, skirt) I got on sale."
  "It must be *nice!*"

Partly out of guilt and partly out of desire, I'd then rummage through my closets to find things I no longer wore. Since Roz and I are the same size, I'd load her up with my castoffs. I am not one of those generous shopaholics who gets off on buying for others. My shopping is pretty selfish.

Another hint of trouble was my obsession with catalogs. Two to six flowed into my mailbox daily, offering everything from gardening tools to diamonds. As soon as I heard the dogs bark, which meant that the mailcarrier was on the way, I'd drift into the kitchen, where I could get an unobstructed view of the mailbox. Once there, I'd plant myself out of view until the second he left. Then I'd slither out the front door and empty our brass-plated mailbox marked "Wesson" (I'd found it in the Horchow catalog!) in one smooth scoop. Heart pounding in anticipation, I'd retreat into the den, sort the boring bills from the slick, glossy catalogs, and sit down for half an hour of pure pleasure.

My bank book balance had declined steadily over the previous two years, but I didn't take that too seriously because I had inherited a lot of money from my deceased husband, and money seemed limitless. Used to living paycheck to paycheck, I suddenly had two hundred thousand dollars. Not only that; I was also playing the stock market with some of this new play money and making more. Without going into all of the tedious details of what I did with the money, I essentially blew about a fourth of it on trips, furniture, art, clothes, and pedigreed dogs.

In the spirit of true confessions, I want to talk about my most outlandish expenditure. But first some background. After my husband died and I remarried, I moved from a roomy, rather run-down, five-bedroom house with two marvelous gardens, into a posh, Spanish-style townhouse. I was very nervous about this change because I love to garden. When I looked out either the den or kitchen window of the new townhouse, I didn't see grass, trees, and flowers, the things I was used to and loved. Instead, I saw a dinky courtyard that had nothing in it but a red tile floor and high, beige-stucco walls. Everyone else in the townhouse development seemed satisfied to just toss a few potted plants here and there. But not me. I was in a panic. How could a gardener ever find happiness in what I took to calling "the prison yard"? There was only one solution. I called in a landscape architect. These guys don't come cheap, but I haggled, and for a mere five hundred dollars he drew up plans for the prison yard as well as the decks. I used exactly one of his magnificent, pricey ideas.

DEATH

It all started in 1983, when my husband, Pat, died of lung cancer. Although he had had cancer for two years, he wasn't incapacitated until about four months before he died. So from all appearances, we led rather normal lives, physically, socially, work-wise. Inside, though, it was awful. Everyone in our family, and I mean *everyone*, denied that Pat was going to die. But I knew the statistics, and I couldn't hide from them. That meant that I was the official reality facer in the family, as well as the one who expressed most of the feelings. I cried all the time, but even so, my stomach twisted into a chronic knot of apprehension. When Pat died, new stresses set in. The kids—in their late teens and early twenties—were a mess, and they acted out their depression in different ways. I was alone and terrified; my best friend and companion of sixteen years was gone.

MORE LOSSES

Depressed and horny, I stormed the singles scene trying to find Pat's replacement. What I got was some good sex and a lot of screwed-up men who I rationalized, were okay, at least in my own mind. Eventually I started meeting some decent guys, but more about that later. First I want to talk about money. When Pat died, I received what I considered to be a lot of money. I was pretty conservative, investing most of it immediately, but I did buy new clothes, took my daughter to Palm Springs and Hawaii, and fixed up the house a little. Yet, inside, I was terrified. I had a secret fear that I'd just go "nutso" one day and do something outrageous.

In his book *Money Madness*, Herb Goldberg talks about the fears I experienced. He explains that sudden wealth commonly makes people fearful, because money raises the underlying, and unconscious, issue of losing control—not just losing control and blowing the money, but losing control of one's feelings, especially hostility and aggression. And, as we saw in chapter 4, maintaining control is a big issue with people who grow up in dysfunctional families.

Two days before Pat died, my mother suffered a severe stroke and wasn't expected to live. Happily, she survived, but she lost most of her memory in recovering. While her basic personality didn't change, the loss of both her short- and long-term memory, paired with her deafness, now makes ongoing meaningful communication with her almost impossible. She and my father were both severely ill on and off the next year, and since I am their only child, it fell to me to fly to them in southern California and to try to handle each crisis. I went five or six times in that next year, but I wasn't much help. I was in too much of a mess myself. I could hardly endure *driving by* a hospital, much less walking into one to see one parent or the other.

During this time, extraordinarily hurtful things started happening with some of my (formerly *our*) best friends. The wife of one couple made it clear, in not too subtle ways, that she didn't want me within a hundred feet of her husband. Another couple was supportive and close until I fell in love; then they grew cool and distant and our relationship collapsed. Another couple just disappeared—poof! Gone! These friends deserted over a period of a year and a half, so I was able to deal with the losses one at a time. Or at least I *thought* I was dealing with them. I would rage, cry, and obsess, and in time the pain seemed to get better. Underneath, I grew more depressed as the losses piled up like shrouded corpses hidden in a dimly lit room.

REMARRIAGE

At the time I remet my current husband, Gil, I had been widowed for about nine months. Gil was a client I had counseled briefly eight years before, and he is the only client for whom I have had anything more than professional feelings. Since he is devastatingly handsome, warm, intelligent, elegant, emotional, and able to talk about his feelings—and show them—it had taken considerable self-control not to pounce. Fortunately, I had remained professional and his counseling ended on a positive and healthy note. Hesitant, he called me nine months after Pat's death, saying he wasn't sure I'd remember him. Hah! How easily would one forget a cross between Alan Alda and Clint Eastwood? We went out on some lovely dates, where I discovered he had the one quality I hoped for most in a future husband—a wonderful, irreverent sense of humor. We fell in love rather speedily, became engaged the following Thanksgiving, and married the next May. When Gil and I started going out, I was still smoking. He hated it. I wanted to quit but was unable to until he issued an ultimatum. He didn't want to marry me if I smoked. I quit within two days, but it was a twenty-year addiction, and I think shopping picked up where cigarettes left off.

Although still grieving for Pat, my kids (my daughter and Pat's son) took to Gil reasonably well, just as Gil's kids did to me. But we each owned a house we dearly loved. Gil's was a wood-and-glass, split-level beauty secluded in the mountains. I loved the house but hated the isolation. Gil wasn't particularly fond of my house and feared he would never develop a sense of belonging there—it would always be *my* house. That's how we ended up in the townhouse, which was a good choice for the relationship but ultimately not good for me. But we couldn't have foreseen that. Gil's house sold in a flash, whereas it took six months for mine to sell. That meant the constant stress of keeping a house full of kids, cats, and dogs perfect. The thing I remember most is running around like a mad woman putting the toilet lids down every time I left the house.

MOVING

The kids moved to their own apartments and Gil and I moved into our beautifully redecorated townhouse. Neither of us had ever had the money before to strip a house down to its underwear and redo every bit of it to our liking. It was great fun, and I was surprised to discover that I had a pretty good eye for decorating. Well, no, actually I'm damn good at it; especially when I have unlimited money. But excerpts from my diary reveal the growing concern I had about my spending:

After lunch with a friend, spot a magnificent, three-strand pearl necklace in a jewelry store window. I admire it, want to show it to Gil. Why do I want it, besides all the obvious reasons? Because it's so exceptional and beautiful it will bring me attention, admiration? Tell Gil, and he suggests I get a beeper that will go off periodically to get attention! Then he hugs me and says, "Oh, do you need attention?" I don't know.

Another source of stress had been simmering for a couple of years—a mini–mid-life crisis about my work. I'd been a therapist for about ten years at that time and wasn't sure I wanted to keep doing it for the rest of my life. But even admitting such feelings seemed like heresy, since I'd spent so many years training for the profession. By now, though, I had co-authored a book and discovered I loved writing. I wrestled with my alternatives and after taking a semester of writing courses decided I didn't have to do one thing or the other. I could still see clients, while satisfying my growing need to do something creative by writing. I toyed with the notion of going into decorating, but after seeing the stress my decorator experienced in dealing with his clients, I decided to pass on that. The last thing I wanted was more stress.

THE BOD FALLS APART

Too bad my body wasn't aware that I needed less stress. I became a walking example of Holmes and Rache's prediction that if we experience too much stress, we can count on our bodies breaking down. The first thing to go was my right shoulder. I was an avid tennis player, and when my right shoulder began hurting, I stupidly ignored the pain. After a long lay off, it still hurt, so I had to have extensive surgery. It was many months before I could play again. I had lost one of my main pleasures in life as well as a chief outlet for stress. Healed at last, I joyfully started playing again.

Played tennis today. My game ends early so I make a beeline for the pro shop. Find a saucy-looking tennis dress. Rationalize buying it by saying it's to celebrate my return to tennis. How's that for ego—like I'm Martina Navratilova. Put it on "hold" so I'll think it over, but I don't really think about it much because I want it, and that's that.

Then a pap smear came back with some class two cell changes, and my excellent but conservative doctor decided to laser beam my cervix to zap anything that might be going awry. But before he could get that scheduled, walking became terribly painful due to little growths in the interior of the balls of my feet. So both growths had to come out, and I was reduced to hobbling around in funny-looking sandals for six weeks. About the time I could have resumed playing tennis, it was time for the cervix procedure, so a few more weeks passed.

Several weeks later, I slipped while walking the dogs, and in the process of righting myself, I tore a ligament in my knee. More surgery, and a long recuperation followed. Anxious and depressed, my shopping increased dramatically, because it was about the only thing I could think to do besides going to work or eating. By now I'd also received a contract to write another book, *Teen Troubles*, which I was writing at home.

Frustrated, want a department store fix. Want to buy something, but we don't need anything. Last night asked Gil to cheer me up by going to our grand and glorious new shopping mall. But I wasn't serious; I just wanted to be distracted and get out of the house. So we went out to dinner instead. Oh good! Just thought of something I need to buy—two towels. Marvelous, and, oh yes, I need makeup, too. Think I'll make a pilgrimage to the new mall this afternoon or tonight. Feel better already.

Now my lower back suffered spasms from a degenerating disc and from the tension I had built up in my body from the trauma of all that surgery in a year and a half. But my body wasn't quite through yet. I was an absolute mess. My diary told the true story:

Very tired. Not sleeping well. Worried about my health. My feet—my stupid feet—have changed sizes three times in the last two years. They have gone from size 10B to 11AAAA. One podiatrist questioned whether or not I have MD or MS. In the middle of the night last night, I went to the guest room to read and hopefully sleep. Gil came in, asked what was wrong, and when I told him, he said, "That is a worry. You'll probably end up with hooves!"

I longed for tennis and began a sensible strengthening program on Nautilus exercise equipment, and after three months I tried it again. No good. My knee swelled each time I played and the pain in my back bent me double afterward. Heartbroken, I finally faced reality and gave up the game. If you love and need sports or activity in your life, you probably can relate to the void this left in my psyche and my life.

Am I spending more in the last few years because I have a lot more money, or is it because I've stopped a huge source of pleasure—tennis? Spent most of the afternoon on a scheme to buy a vacation/rental home in Belize, Central America. Made many phone calls. Good distraction. May or may not be a very good investment strategy, but I have to wonder if the whole thing isn't related to anxiety. Also, what about my need for change all the time?

TAX TIME

Three more events converged during this health crisis, and I came within a whisker of a nervous breakdown. I didn't go nuts, lose touch with reality, or otherwise become psychotic—I just felt like screaming. But I'm getting ahead of myself. First came a meeting with our accountant, who informed us that we were going to have to give the feds ten thousand dollars in tax money. This was a blow. Up to that point, I had always gotten money *back* from the government. Now I had to give *them* money for little apparent reason,

: fact that we had a lovely income. This is where
:uckoo thinking blazed forth in screaming techni-
)ught nothing of blowing hundreds of dollars a
clothes, thousands on vacations, furniture, and art.
It killed me, though, to pay our fair share of taxes. So my
scheming, manipulative, and canny mind launched into a four-
month program of ways to shelter our income. I think I was
really worried about my own spending but parlayed that into
worry about this wasteful business of paying the government.
So I researched, consulted, figured, obsessed, and lost sleep
figuring out the best way to protect our capital.

My solution was to buy a lovely little vacation rental in
Hawaii—preferably Kauai, since it was relatively undeveloped.
Gil and I flew over to the islands for a quick real estate buy.
We found a beautiful condo. The price was right, and we
made an offer. Unfortunately, the owner was Bunker Hunt, of
the Hunt billionaire family and one of the brothers who
allegedly tried to corner the silver market of the world. Initially
that added a dash of glamor to the whole deal, but it turned
out that Hunt neither looked at nor responded to our offer
for about three months. Since we were buying this place for a
write-off (depreciation, etc.), the delay was not only frustrating, enraging, and enough to drive everyone involved nuts; it
was also costing us money.

While this torturous deal dragged on, my therapy practice partners and I decided to move our professional offices to
a new building. I was in charge of the deal, which meant that
I was usually the one who talked to the architect and the
contractor. It turned out that the contractor had a disagree-
ment with the architect, or the owner of the building, or
someone, and I had trouble working with him from the first
minute we met him. It seemed to me that he did not deal well
with women on a professional level. We finally refused to talk
to him, and an intermediary transmitted communications.
The construction of our offices took about three months—the
same three months that the Hawaiian condo deal was going
nowhere, so I was plastered to the ceiling with anxiety. I was

enraged at these grossly inconsiderate men, but being the educated, reasoning, professional, and ladylike woman that I pretended to be, I didn't scream out my frustration. I stayed relatively calm, carried on until we found another condo, turned over the office to my one partner who wasn't at the end of her rope, and fell apart.

LOSING IT

It happened one Tuesday as I was walking up the stairs to the old office to see the clients I had scheduled that day. Suddenly I was struck with an uncontrollable urge to scream. Certainly I'd felt like screaming before, but it had always been a fleeting feeling. This time it wouldn't go away, and I had no sense that I could control myself. Hastily I stuck a note on the door of my office telling my clients I'd gotten sick—true, actually—and fled down the street to *my* psychiatrist's office. He squeezed me in between other patients, reassured me that I wasn't going nuts, and strongly suggested I take some time off work. Relieved, I did just what he said and took three months off work—and off life. During this time I wrote a little, lay in the hammock, read books, and went to see my shrink. I didn't want to talk to anyone but good friends, and I could hardly walk the dogs down the street without anxiety. It turned out that this fear of screaming actually had been caused by a severe hormonal imbalance that kicked in when I switched from progesterone to estrogen pills.

During this time off, I don't remember thinking about much of anything. Instead, I took full advantage of the luxury of just considering what I wanted to do that morning, that afternoon, that evening. I consciously blocked out all thoughts of the next week, next month, or the future, because it was my constant worrying and trying to control people and events in the future that had gotten me into such emotional trouble. Slowly it began to sink in that even if I decided to continue on the same, self-destructive path, it would do me no good because so much of the future was out of my hands. About the only thing I had the slightest control over was myself, and even that was dubious. I also learned to "let go" because any serious thoughts or worries were so noxious that I would mentally squash them the minute they surfaced. I simply couldn't handle anything serious.

My psychiatrist put me on antidepressants, because they work so well in reducing anxiety and because I was depressed. The latter came as a complete surprise because I had no awareness of depression. When I was writing my previous book, *Teen Troubles,* thoughts of suicide would dart through my mind, but I chalked that up to the fact that I was writing about teenagers' depressions and suicides, not mine. Somewhere deep inside, I knew that my recurring thoughts about suicide were a symptom of depression, but I whipped out my shield of denial and thought, Nah, not me. What did I have to be depressed about? I was very happily married, had a gorgeous home, my kids were okay, and my work was interesting. What more could I want?

DENIAL

There *was* that little problem of my friends' having abandoned me, but that would heal in time, I rationalized. Somehow I'd make new friends—friends who could talk honestly with me about problems in our relationship so that we could fix things rather than just kiss off our friendship.

My wreck of a body was a problem, but surely nothing more could go wrong, at least not for a while. Besides, Gil and I had joined a golf club, and I could make it around nine holes without anything hurting. I found the game tedious, but I enjoyed the deer and rabbits that meandered onto the course. Maybe I could find a way to like the game and get physical activity back into my life.

Our house. Better not think about *that.* Gil loved it, we'd sunk about fifteen thousand into upgrades, and I did put in that brick planter so that I'd have one place I could actually turn over some dirt. I loved my neighbors, loved standing around in the middle of the cul-de-sac shooting the breeze with them on the weekends, loved the fact that I could call about six or seven people if I needed something. But God, I missed my yard and gardening. There was no green lawn, no bushes begging to be trimmed, flowers to change with the seasons, brush to haul around to the side of the house and somehow cram into garbage cans. No dirt under my fingernails, no bugs to marvel at, no worms to save.

Then there were my parents, my poor parents. They live four hundred miles away, and there wasn't much I could do. I tried not to think about my mother in the nursing home, my father's heartbreak, and the fact that my father was depressed and saying off-the-wall stuff now and then. I've never been able to confront my father, but this was not the time to try, I said to myself. Better forget about the whole situation for the time being.

And Gil. My beloved Gil turned out to be a couch potato, compelled to read the newspaper from beginning to end, one eye glued to the TV. I bitched, moaned, and pleaded, with limited success. He wanted to stay rooted to the damned couch and watch TV all weekend, while I wanted to play, to party, *to get out of the house!* And at times he was extraordinarily parental with me, which I just hate. I'll just have to figure out a way to live with this stuff, I decided. I'm certainly not perfect, and besides, he could give *courses* in lovemaking. I can't expect to have it all.

As you can see, I had a lot not to think about, which is why I went shopping.

Thankfully, my therapist, Phil Kavanaugh, didn't let me continue to groom my ostrichlike feathers. He'd just recently traveled the road of anxiety and depression himself and had found a way out through twelve-step programs, such as Al-Anon and Adult Children of Alcoholics (ACA). His work with me was two-pronged: by introducing me to the life-generating process of working a twelve-step program, he showed me how to live more happily *each day*. At the same time, he encouraged me to confront the people and the troubles I wanted to ignore.

CONFRONTATIONS

My dad was the first one to get it. He has mellowed with age, but the little girl in me still wanted to avoid his unpredictable anger at all costs. I really hadn't taken him on since I was a college student, when we made politics our battlefield. He'd accuse my professors of corrupting me with "left-wing, pinko talk." I'd hurl back specifics of America's inane foreign policy, and we'd gleefully draw our swords. In retrospect, I think he probably saw my repudiation of his political values as a rejection of him, while I used our growing differences as a covert way of declaring my independence. I was never able to summon up the courage to say, "I don't like the way you're acting right now."

By the time I stumbled into Phil's office, I had a short list of grievances against my dad, and Phil felt it was crucial that I slay the dragon of my fear—not my father, just the terror of speaking my truth to him. During my childhood, my father struggled with some enervating problems of his own: my mother's alcoholism and agoraphobia, work in the building business, a notoriously combative field, his painful back, and periods of depression. He had plenty to feel angry about, but I, as a child, did not understand any of this. He was simply my wonderful, adoring father, who would blow up without apparent cause. His anger terrified my insecure mother and scared me. Interestingly, it wasn't until just recently that I learned that my mother was an alcoholic until I was eleven. I had always believed she stopped drinking when I was five, and therefore thought I never suffered any ill effects from her drinking. I probably was not aware when my mother drank, because my mental picture of her throughout my life is one of her either sitting or lying down on the living room couch. She was always sweet, loving, wonderful to talk to, and very passive. To this day I am completely unaware of any change in her personality when she drank, which suggests that I've got a lot of denial operating about this period of my life. If I were to express my impressions of my parents on paper, my mother would be kind of soft and hazy and my father would be vivid and intense. That's why he has had such an impact on me.

Phil helped me realize that my father was no longer the powerful, sometimes terrifying, authority figure of my childhood, but an aging man who might *need me*. What a startling thought.

Emboldened with this novel concept of equality with my father, I wrote him a letter, carefully and, I hoped, kindly, laying out my grievances. I closed the letter saying it was not necessary for us to talk about the letter or its contents. After I mailed the letter, I experienced twenty-four hours of euphoria and strength. Then anxiety set in. I was worried he'd call in a rage and we'd have some horrible argument that would end in bitter recriminations. A few days later he did call, and in a warm but indirect way let me know he understood my feelings.

In *The Dance of Anger* Harriet Lerner writes at length about our need to separate emotionally from our parents and the anxiety that that produces. By her explanation, I was feeling separation anxiety, *"a disturbing sense of separateness and aloneness that we experience when we make our difference known."* (Italics added.) Separation anxiety comes from an underlying discomfort with separateness and individuality. It has it roots in our early family experiences, where the unspoken rule was not to express our negative feelings. Daughters, Lerner believes, are especially sensitive to such demands and become far more skilled at protecting the relational "we" than asserting the autonomous "I." She also declares again and again how important it is for us to settle differences, or to set limits with people in our first family, so that we can then move on to our contemporary relationships. If we avoid confronting people from our childhood, we condemn ourselves to carrying around underlying anxieties that accompany those unexpressed feelings.

Because of the focus of this book, I've painted a picture of my father that is one-dimensional—the child's picture of a powerful parent. I haven't told you that he is warm, generous, always supportive, bright, witty, friendly, and utterly devoted to my mother and the people he loves. He's also a poet, a gardener, a man of mathematics, and the "father" of Gladys, his sumptuous Angora cat, who, like my mother, receives gourmet treatment from him.

After dealing with my dad, my self-esteem puffed up and I was damn proud of myself. In fact, I was on a roll, and my husband got temporarily flattened in the process. I mentioned earlier that he can be critical and parental. Ordinarily I just tell him to "stick it," and we get along fine. But one afternoon after my partners and I moved into our new offices, Gil came over and scolded me loudly about something I had done that had bugged him. What sent me over the edge was not his anger, but the fact that he had hollered at me *in my place of business*. We went home, I cried for two hours (a lot of those tears had nothing to do with the situation), and the next day I called my attorney. In an ice-cold rage, I instructed him to put all of my separate property in my name only. Then I changed the brokerage accounts to my name. I told Gil that no one would ever be allowed to speak to me that way again, especially in public. Exactly how I connected changing all of my property to my name with his behavior I'm not sure. I think I was simply underscoring the fact that I was becoming tough, and he'd better not mess with me in that way. I was taking another step toward setting limits with people close to me, but my behavior was highly reactive rather than thought out. Eventually I changed everything back to both of our names, but Gil had gotten the point.

Next I took on a very good friend, Mercedes. She's a tall, beautiful, sweet woman, a codependent who learned her need for control from her mother, perhaps the most controlling woman I have ever met. In an effort to be helpful (controlling), Mercedes would slip into the critical parent role with me, and I hated it. Her parenting usually took the form of questioning that was supposed to lead me to the "right" thought or behavior. Fed up, I eventually refused to answer her questions, saying flat-out, "I'm not going to answer that question," by which I really meant, "It's none of your concern,

I'm grown up, and I'll handle it as I see best." Finally she scolded me once too often, and I said that I didn't want a parent-child relationship with my friends. I spelled out just what was bugging me and told her I wanted a "sabbatical" from our relationship. I ended by saying, "I hope I can work through whatever my end of the problem is and we can pick up our friendship at a later date." Understandably defensive, she wished me luck in solving "my problem," and that friendship screeched to a halt for about a year and a half.

In a sense, she was right. I did work through my problem—I realized that I hated my friend's controlling behavior because it was so much like mine. I was perhaps more subtle about it, but we were bumping heads because of our similarities, not our differences. In time I grew to miss her. I called her up and she graciously agreed to resume our friendship. Our relationship is not as intense as it was a couple of years ago, but it's a lot healthier.

TURNING POINT

I haven't talked about my shopping during this period, primarily because I can't really remember that anything significant was changing. I don't think I was spending a bunch on clothes, but I was shopping like a fiend for the new condo we finally bought in Hawaii. Although it was furnished, I wanted it to look terrific so that the managing company would be more inclined to rent it and so that renters would return. That turned out to be a good business maneuver, but it was also a lovely excuse to keep shopping. Eventually I sent over sixteen boxes of pictures, bedspreads, kitchen items, books, and so on.

Come to think of it, I *was* still buying clothes, but my focus was on just one thing. My stepson Ward (Pat's son) was getting married, and I was on the hunt for the "perfect" dress. I had a couple hanging in my closet that would do, but I wasn't about to settle for something ordinary. I wanted something striking and jaunty (no matronly mother-of-the-groom number for me). I bought and returned at least five or six dresses before I finally found a six hundred–dollar beauty at I. Magnin—hand-painted coral silk with a slightly ethnic look (I'm a sucker for ethnic). I justified the outrageous price by saying to Gil (who never criticizes my clothes spending but is still somehow my external conscience) that "it was my reward for raising Ward since he was seven years old." Not bad, as excuses go. As a matter of fact, I am an expert at rationalization. My friends call me up when they're feeling guilty about something, and I can rattle off four or five rationalizations without even giving the matter serious thought.

Ward's wedding was a mega-stress affair, partly because of Ward's stepfamily situation. Even though I had raised Ward since he was seven, a couple of people seemed to think I should slink off to the back pew of the church during his wedding, since I was not his *biological* mother. Incensed, but used to this kind of sabotage for twenty years, I stood my ground, right there in front pew center. Unresolved issues with a member of my late husband's family also bubbled over at one of the prenuptial events. Still on my assertive roll, I said some things that had been festering for years, and initially I felt better. This was a couple of days before the wedding, so unfortunately, I added to the tension. The following is from my diary, written the day after the wedding:

> *I thought my recovery from shopaholism would be abrupt; one day I'd wake up cured. But, of course, it isn't like that. I think I'm in recovery, but my changing is a slippery thing: one day forward, the next day back. Ward's wedding seems like a milestone. After frantically looking for the perfect dress for six months—so I'd be the "star" mother, that's what it was all about—suddenly the day before the wedding it no longer mattered a whit! Was it connected to purging myself of the hurt and anger I've felt toward Pat's relative? Or was it simply the awareness that, if I took back my gorgeous but extravagant six hundred–dollar dress, which I did, Gil and I could buy a lot of dinners in Hawaii with that money. No, I*

think it was more than common sense. It was self-respect, self-honoring such that I no longer needed yards of hand-painted silk to be acceptable. I and my old dress (with a smidgen of new jewelry), were ADEQUATE! I didn't have to win the best-dressed contest because there was none. It was all in my head, my fearful adolescent hangover.

After the wedding, Gil and I went to Hawaii to stay in our new condominium for the first time. That sounds terrific, but it wasn't peachy every minute. The first couple of days were exciting and wonderful as we preened and admired our condominium. But, then we started acting like tense, nervous homeowners instead of people on a vacation, and we fought and had a crummy time the first week. Finally, we knocked off the compulsive homeowners bit and started having fun, but we almost ruined the whole vacation with our anxieties.

I had another unspoken anxiety. Every time I looked at our beautiful home, it hit me that if I didn't get a grip on my spending, we might lose it. That recognition provided a powerful motivation to cut back. A few months before, as I was reading Earnie Larsen's *Stage II Recovery, Life Beyond Addiction,* I had come upon this paragraph: "In my experience, we do not change *until we have some kind of awakening to the fact that we are going to lose something we are not prepared to live without if we do not change.*" (Italics mine.) He calls this awakening a conversion experience. That statement is a little strong for me. I could live without the condo, but I wouldn't like myself if we lost it because of my excessive spending.

My turning point evolved from the convergence of these events—setting limits with Pat's relatives, realizing I didn't need a fancy dress for Ward's wedding, and visiting our condo. Each brought about an internal change in my attitudes toward money that stuck.

PLEASURE HUNT

When I faced the fact that I could no longer play tennis, I knew I had to find something to replace it. That meant figuring out other things that made me happy. Since shopping and buying clothes didn't really do it, except for about ten minutes, I eliminated them from my thinking. Here's a partial reconstruction of the things I did think of: (1) snorkeling and body surfing; (2) gardening; (3) drum and bugle corps shows; (4) playing with the dogs; (5) riding horses—I hadn't done that in ten years; (6) sex; and (7) reading.

Snorkeling and body surfing are wonderful, but they're possible only when we go on vacations, so that wouldn't do much for me on a daily basis. Gardening, except in the most limited way, was out. Drum and bugle corps shows are only performed in the summer, so that left the rest of the year blank. I love romping and cuddling with my dogs, so I began allowing myself more time to do that. Some mornings I'll stay in bed for half an hour, and like a big kid, dive under the covers and let the dogs try to dig me out with their licks and nuzzling. Horseback riding, hmmm. It had been years since I'd last done it with any regularity, but I had loved it then. I'd loved galloping around the open fields, sometimes with confidence, other times just barely hanging on, and I'd never forgotten the exhilaration. Sex is terrific, but I didn't think Gil would quit his job and stay home and make love all day, so that wasn't very practical. Since I already read a great deal, reading even more didn't seem that appealing.

I decided to try horseback riding again, but felt I needed some lessons, because I couldn't remember how to steer a horse or how to get it to stop. The first Saturday morning I went for a group lesson I was fearful of the horses, afraid I wouldn't be any good at it (God forbid), but excited nonetheless. It's turned out to be wonderful.

I now take English dressage lessons privately every other week (fifteen dollars), which I find challenging, frustrating, and exciting. I'm also leasing a horse, Daisy (one hundred dollars a month), whom I adore, even though she's bitten my behind and stepped on my feet. I love the slow, curvy drive through the foothills to get to the stables, and I relish the atmosphere once I get there. Everyone is dressed in grubbies, because you get filthy riding, brushing, and grooming horses and stepping in manure. I love it all, and I even get a little charge out of the horsy smell of my clothes and car. The stables have cats, dogs, roosters, and chickens wandering around, so there's always something to pet. Although I'm very cautious around Daisy and the other horses, I kind of like the risk involved as well. That fits in with what Joy Davidson says in *The Agony of It All*. For me, riding is high excitement.

As much as riding fulfilled my need for excitement and stimulation, it wasn't doing a thing for my body tone: my cellulite and the mud-slide effect of my skin, sagging its way down to the floor. Something had to be done about that, but what? Between the problems with my feet, knee, and back, there was little I could do. My partner, Ann, was going to yoga classes and just loving it. She, too, is a mild wreck, so I figured that if she could do it, perhaps I could, too. I've been going two or three times a week now, and it's become an absolute must in my life. There are many different kinds of yoga; the class I go to is called hatha yoga. I'm not sure what that means, but it's a very gentle type of stretching and strengthening, which is slowly reshaping my body. I didn't know then that yoga has other aspects to it that I desperately needed. First, it teaches me how to stay focused on what I'm doing at that very moment and how to shut my mind off, which reduces anxiety. At the same time there's a spiritual aspect to the process that focuses on our "oneness" with the universe and underscores the processes of taking in warmth and love and giving it out. This sounds like something from the late sixties and, in a way, I suppose it is, although yoga's been around for centuries. Without raving on much more, I'll say that I've found it to be a fine blend of conditioning, relaxation, focusing, and learning to live moment by moment. All of these things I'm going to have to practice the rest of my life.

Both riding and yoga serve another crucial function. They get me out of the house on the weekends, when Gil is rooted to the couch. He is a satellite operations engineer and has been closely involved with the space program for a number of years. He has several early morning meetings a week, which leaves him tired on the weekends. But, equally important, he is certifiably addicted to TV! So, Saturday mornings I go to yoga, Sundays I ride for a couple of hours in the afternoon. Finding things to do on my own that I truly enjoy and can do without resentment has cut down a lot on arguments. Again, from *The Dance of Anger:* "As we learn to relinquish responsibility for the self, we are prone to blame others for failing to fill up our emptiness or provide for our happiness—which is not their job."

Without conscious thought or decision, I've found other activities that Gil and I both love. We've added them to our lives since I quit shopping excessively. I love music but had not been to the symphony since I was a child. A few months ago we went and were enchanted. The music was primarily Russian, wonderfully melodic. Since then we have gone many times, and I even have a favorite piece that I rave about to anyone I can corner: Beethoven's *Wellington's Victory,* Opus 91. Besides the beauty of the music that first night, the whole affair was electrifying. First of all I got to dress up, which I adore. The orchestra, dressed in black dresses or tails, warmed up for about fifteen minutes, and as they did, I found myself scooting closer and closer to the edge of my seat. The orchestra's excitement and delight in their music radiated out to the restless and murmuring audience, and anticipation grew. Finally, the conductor strode out from the wings, bowed to the audience, acknowledged the applause, took the podium, and, with elegant, subtle movements, seized control of everyone in the hall. Mesmerized and enchanted, neither of us wanted the evening to end. For Christmas this year I have asked for a series of concert tickets that will enable us to go to six concerts at the beautiful Marion Davies Hall in San Francisco for about $240 for the two of us—not cheap, but then neither is shopping.

I mentioned earlier in the chapter that I felt that a metamorphosis had taken place in my life, and I want to talk

more about that. But first some background. As we discussed
earlier, the brain is divided into two hemispheres, left and
right. The left side is where our logical and judgmental
thinking takes place, while the right side is responsible for our
more intuitive and creative thinking. Engineering, for instance, is a left-brain activity, while painting is directed by the
right side of the brain. Most of my life I had been involved in
activities that required using the left side of my brain. Although doing therapy requires some right-brain activity, such
as intuition, it mostly demands highly logical and intellectual
thinking, a left-brain discipline. Even my favorite play activity,
tennis, is a "heady" game, because it relies so much on
strategy.

When I began writing six years ago, I activated more and
more of the right side of my brain. I discovered that the more
I dwelt in the right house of my brain, the happier I was. One
time in my own therapy I was talking about this, and it
dawned on me that both sides of my family have worked in
right-brain, or creative, occupations. On my mom's side, my
grandfather, great-uncle, and great-grandfather were archi-
tects. On my father's side, my great-great-grandfather and my
great-grandfather were nurserymen in England. My grandfather was a florist and a cofounder of FTD. My grandmother
was an actress. Both of my parents write. So my gene pool is
jam-packed with creativity (and a bunch of eccentrics). In an
interview, Marion Woodward, a Jungian analyst, discusses the
connection between creativity and addiction, stating, *"I don't
know any way out of it if you don't have a creative outlet. You have
to find your own way of expressing yourself."*

As my shopping has decreased, I feel as though a new
creative and adventurous part of my personality has surfaced,
unconsciously leading me to a richer and far more satisfying
life. I still shop, still get change-of-season anxiety about the
deficits in my wardrobe, but as I've grown to realize that
money is indeed limited, my spending's shifted to things that
enrich my life and satisfy my soul.

I will talk more about the practical strategies I've found

to cut down on my shopping in chapter 10. Here I want to focus on the core changes I've made in myself and in my relationships. As Earnie Larsen puts it in *Stage II Recovery: Life Beyond Addiction:*

> How did our lives come to need rebuilding? In what context did all that pain come to be? Since few of us are hermits, the unsurprising answer lies in the social context—the world of personal relationships in which each of us lives and breathes and has had our being since birth. We get sick in the company of other people and we get well in the company of other people. There is no other way it could be. I believe that learning to make relationships work is the core of full recovery.

UPDATE

Since the preceding material was written over the last year, several more changes have taken place that have brought about peace of mind and a great step toward full self-confidence. The loss of some of my friendships plagued me daily because I never knew what had gone wrong. So one Friday afternoon, I called up each former friend and asked to discuss our problems. In each case, what had gone wrong were small misunderstandings that mushroomed because they were never discussed. I have resumed my friendships with the two couples I loved the most, and I am at peace with a third friend's rejection. I'm no longer hopelessly trying to understand all of those unanswered questions and unresolved hurts that were spinning in my brain.

In my relationship with Gil, my goal has been steadfast: to make our relationship happy. To do that, I wrongly short-changed some of my own needs, and I almost fell into that God-awful Phyllis Schlafly trap of "keep your man happy and you'll be happy, too." Not so. I bring this up because, as I began focusing on what made me happy, I realized that I had given up too many things that mattered to me. For instance, I generally hate the racket of TV and dislike most of the programs. I would much prefer music or quiet. But Gil loves TV and has it on all the time. I not only found that annoying, but most often it prevented me from being able to listen to the music I love, because the television and the compact disc player and speakers are all in the den. When Gil feels cornered, he, too, threatens and intimidates, so when it came to negotiation of some issues like watching TV or listening to music, I fell back into my lifelong pattern of capitulation and quiet resentment. It was only when I assessed what made me happy that I realized how sorely I missed listening to music.

From that came a compromise that will meet both Gil's needs and mine. Upstairs we have a room that I use for writing. We're going to convert it into Gil's sanctuary, where he will have the things that matter to him. Another TV will go in there, as will his computer and all of the other things that he enjoys. The downstairs den will become mine, so to speak, in that the TV won't go on unless it's okay with me. I can also turn up my music without disturbing Gil. An obvious resolution to a thorny problem, but one that would never have come about had I not taken stock of the things that bring me joy.

I've also found some more places to garden, because I've expanded my territory into the entryway of our townhouse, and onto some little strips of land we share with neighbors. So now I have four places to mess in the dirt, and I'm completely satisfied. That's partly because I also have my own horse, Sweet William, and caring for him and riding him take many hours a week. Once again my life is full of the things that truly matter to me: strenuous activity, gardens, sunshine, music, and dirt. It never would have happened if I hadn't figured out what I really needed and taken a stand. I've done the same thing with my relationships. I've weeded out the unhealthy ones and am left with those in which respect and mutual kindness are the centerpiece. I will never again settle for anything less.

Part Three

How to Quit

Chapter 9

Getting Ready for Change: New Ways to Handle Your Feelings

In this chapter, I'll focus on feelings and how we handle them. Since feelings often reflect our pasts, we tend to think we can only change our current feelings if we can understand our pasts through insight. But, it is equally true that if we decide to *act* differently, regardless of our feelings, our changed behavior will soon become the new basis for what we feel. Let me give you an example. Many people fear heights and, because of that fear, avoid high places. If they decide, however, that they'd like to get over their fear, they may systematically expose themselves to taller and taller buildings, becoming comfortable with each new height as they practice. In time they can look at a balcony on a twenty-story building, for instance, and say to themselves, no problem. I've felt comfortable in buildings this tall and even taller. Thus their behavior changed their feelings about heights, rather than the other way around.

The same thing can happen with other feelings. If you change how you *act* and keep at it long enough, behaving in a healthy manner will be as comfortable as acting in a self-defeating manner used to be. Shopping is a Band-Aid that we can gently peel off as we expose our wounds to the fresh air of more satisfying alternatives.

ANGER

Unhealthy Ways of Expressing Anger

When we're momentarily angry at our husbands or lovers, it can be extremely gratifying to storm out to the stores and shop like fiends or call up a catalog place and order a gorgeous new outfit. Having thus righted the wrongs done to us, it's easier to forgive our spouses because we've secretly evened the score. But then we've got a problem of what to do with our purchases. If we're feeling strong and defiant, we might whip our treasures out of their bags and wave them under our husbands' noses. But usually we don't. Instead, we sweep into the house self-satisfied, innocent, and empty-handed, because we've hidden our bounty in the trunks of our cars. But hiding is very damaging. It forces us into sins of omission and sins of commission, and this takes a toll on our self-esteem. We feel deceitful hiding things and guilty when we lie. Further, it puts us in a little girl role with our big, bad husbands.

Sometimes anger directed at a spouse is long-standing, and we get stuck handling our feelings in the same old ineffective ways. When Deena was interviewed for this book, she rated her marriage as happy, yet when asked about her husband she described him as a couch potato who is addicted to television, sports, cigarettes, work, and gardening. He is also a quiet man, she stated, so they don't talk much. When asked what one feeling sent her out shopping, she replied, "Fights with my husband." Deena is one of the most highly addicted shoppers I interviewed, and I believe that her problems stem primarily from her unhappiness with her marriage, although her dissatisfaction seems to be largely unconscious.

Deena obsessively thinks about shopping, even when she is working at her job in the warehouse of an electronics plant. A crafts fair junkie, she shops every single weekend. She gets ready for her shopping safaris on Friday nights by outfitting her backpack with all the things she'll need for the weekend: comfortable shoes, a sweater in case it gets chilly, and snacks to get her through each day. She leaves early Saturday and Sunday mornings and doesn't return home until after sundown. This way she neatly avoids confronting the hurt and anger she may feel at her totally preoccupied husband.

Acting out her unexpressed anger has cost Deena the twenty-thousand dollars she inherited from her parents. Now that this source of money is gone, she is running up her credit cards and beginning to worry about her spending.

For many years therapists have encouraged their clients to show their anger. During the sixties, for instance, people were encouraged to get it out, no matter what the cost (short of abuse and murder, of course). Not only were people encouraged to feel and get angry, but they were encouraged to do it with *gusto*. If you felt like yelling, then you were supposed to yell—loud . . . louder!

Other therapists, however, took a look at the consequences of this uninhibited expression of anger and found damaging results. They learned that unrestrained rage breaks down barriers within us, so we're more apt to go overboard, not just this time, but time and time again. Also, our unleashed anger acts as a model for the people around us to let loose their rage, so we end up in destructive screaming matches.

Yet, unexpressed anger is equally damaging. When we're angry, our body kicks in adrenalin, which prepares us for two responses—to fight or to flee. When anger is expressed through flight, we turn tail, slam doors, leave the house, and avoid the problem that caused our anger. Yet if we do *nothing,* the adrenaline eventually transforms itself into unproductive energy and twists itself into many shapes and symptoms that must be released. It may come out as a migraine headache, hypertension, depression, ulcers, skin problems, sexual dysfunction, or allergies. If it doesn't use one or more of those escape routes, the anger lies dormant in our bodies. *It never goes away entirely.*

Why We Avoid Our Anger

In *The Dance of Anger,* Harriet Lerner suggests that if our ways of managing anger aren't working, it's probably because we've fallen into one of two categories: the "bitch" group, in which we get mad with ease but participate in ineffective fighting, or, more likely, the "nice lady" group. We stay silent and become either tearful, self-critical, or hurt instead of angry. When we're nice, our energy is directed toward protecting the other person and preserving harmony in our relationship. "We behave as if having a relationship is more important than having a self," says Lerner. To make that possible, we convert our anger into guilt. "If we feel *guilty* about not giving enough, or not doing enough for others, it is unlikely we will be angry about not getting enough. . . . Nothing, but nothing, will block the awareness of anger so effectively as guilt and self-doubt. . . . Many of us still feel guilty if we are anything less than an emotional service station to others."

When we submerge our anger in this way, we may not feel it, but others do. They can sense it and cut a wide path around us. We are avoided because our anger sneaks out in passive-aggressive behaviors. Examples: forgetting a close friend's birthday; repeatedly saying untactful things; becoming cold and aloof without explaining why; frequently burning our spouse's dinner; forgetting to pass on messages; not repaying debts. And, of course, shopping.

Old Anger

When anger lingers, it expresses itself in different forms until it's finally put to rest. Sometimes we unconsciously re-create past situations that we know will make us angry so we can end them differently this time and finally get rid of the old anger. If the source of your anger is an old situation, something that dates back to your childhood, say, you might want to get some professional help figuring out how to handle it constructively. Anger left over from our childhoods is especially thorny because we also have a lot of little girl fears about expressing that anger, even though we're adults.

Current Anger

Since much of the anger that fuels excessive shopping comes from our current relationships, it is imperative that we become honest with ourselves. It's always tempting to flick unpleasant feelings out of our lives, but, as we've seen, it doesn't work. Sooner or later, we need to face the fact that we're pissed. At the same time, it is reassuring to know that we have the choice of just feeling our feelings and not necessarily acting on them at that moment. In many cases the most appropriate response to our own anger is to do nothing—at least not right away. This is especially true with rage. If we wait long enough, usually about ten to twenty minutes, it will subside. The body can produce only so much adrenaline before exhaustion sets in. While the adrenaline is coursing through our bodies, it's important to do something physical with it—get out the vacuum and clean the hell out of the rugs; go outside and pull weeds; fast-walk, jog, or run. Then, when we're feeling calmer, we can deal with our feelings productively.

After we've cooled down, we need to express our angry feelings to ourselves using behavioral words as much as possible. For example, if you feel that your husband neglects you, spell out exactly what that means. For example: "When Brent stays at the office until eight o'clock, I feel his work is more important than I am." Stating things in behavioral terms will help us define rather than blame. Blaming ourselves or others gets us nowhere, because it's a delaying tactic that focuses our attention on who's at fault rather than what can be changed to resolve the problem.

How to Express Anger Directly

Once you're clear about the behavior that's bothering you, talk it over with the person involved. This is the hardest part for most people, so here are some hints: always talk about *your feelings* rather than the other person's personality or traits. Using the previous example, Brent's wife would say "I have a problem when you stay at the office until eight. *I feel* as though your job is more important to you than I am." All too often we start conversations in just the opposite manner, saying something like: *"You don't give a damn about me!* You care more about your stupid job than you do about me." Phrasing problems assertively (first example) rather than aggressively or reproachfully (second example) makes it much easier for your husband, or whoever, to hear what's bothering you. You're not putting him or her on the defensive. If you want to make sure you're communicating assertively, picture your index finger pointing either toward yourself or toward your spouse. If you're talking about him and his misdeeds, your finger's figuratively pointed at him. If you're talking about your own feelings, it's pointed at you. That's where it should be.

When Expressing Anger Directly Doesn't Work

If you express your feelings and nothing changes, you have two alternatives. The first one is to use a technique called word pictures. People have been using word pictures for centuries, but two Arizona psychotherapists, Gary Smalley and John Trent, have polished and elaborated this ancient technique into a contemporary communication tool. They thoroughly explain it in *The Language of Love,* part of which is reprinted here with permission from *Focus on the Family Publishing,* copyright © 1988. Here is the basic idea: because the left hemisphere of men's brains is larger and more developed than their right, they tend to focus on the actual words that are being said to them, and miss the underlying emotions. Women do the opposite, because they are more often right-brained. We tune in to nonverbal expression and note the emotional content of what's being said more than the actual words. Since men may be a little dense when it comes to hearing feelings, one has to activate the right side of their brains to get through to them. Conversely, if a man wants to communicate effectively with his wife, he needs to reach her emotionally as well as logically.

To communicate effectively with your husband/lover, you may need to draw word pictures that trigger an emotional response. You do this by drawing an analogy between what you're feeling and some experience or object he can relate to. Let's use the example of the man mentioned above, Brent, who works late. First, his spouse identifies a hobby, interest, or cause that Brent is interested in. Let's say he loves trains. His wife then describes her feelings of anger and rejection by using a story about trains.

The scenario might go something like this: "I feel like an old stationmaster at the depot downtown. You're a shiny, new, high-tech freight train that is scheduled to stop here at 5:17 P.M. Every evening I dust off my uniform, polish my badge, straighten my hat, pick up my red flag, and proudly stride out to the tracks to flag you down. I listen intently for the rumble of your wheels and squint my eyes to see if I can catch a glimpse of your glistening engine. As you finally draw closer, I stand a little straighter because soon you're going to come to a halt in *my station*. But when I finally get you in my sights, something sinks inside me, because I don't hear the shriek of your brakes. You don't slow down. You just flash by the station, ignoring my frantically waving flag, and roar down the tracks. Slowly I walk back to the station, feeling sad and angry, and think to myself, Well, maybe tomorrow night."

Other clues about the use of word pictures: be sure to use good timing. If you husband's a TV addict, talk to him during a time you're not going to compete with his favorite show or a football game. If your spouse doesn't seem to be much interested in anything besides TV, use one of his favorite programs or his favorite sports team to form your word picture. If you're still at a loss, find out what he liked as a child or notice what he loathes as an adult. Another idea would be to find out what motivates him to work overtime. Is it fear, ambition, money or, perhaps recognition?

When you've talked to your spouse in a clear, nonjudgmental manner, you can expect one of the following responses:

1. He agrees, *he wants* to change his behavior, and he follows through.

2. He agrees, *he wants* to change his behavior, and he makes reasonable, but spotty, attempts to change.

3. He says *he is happy with his behavior* and doesn't want to change.

4. He *says* he'll change his behavior, but he doesn't.

If you get the first response, you're in luck. Your anger will dissipate slowly as you see his behavior change. The second response is not quite as positive, but it is realistic. Few of us can change our behavior without a struggle. Instead, it takes a fairly long time and we flip-flop back and forth between what we're trying to change and habit. Show your husband your appreciation for his *attempts* to change, not just his successes. That lets him know that you are aware how hard it is to change. Also note that some people feel patronized when you compliment them for their good behavior; they feel evaluated rather than genuinely complimented.

CHANGING BEHAVIOR

Your Husband's or Lover's Behavior

If your husband is clear about not wanting to change, at least you've gotten a straight answer and you can decide what to do. The same is true for response number four, except that your husband wasn't as clear about it. Still, the next move is up to you. If you find his behavior unacceptable, then try to use your disappointment and anger to *establish your bottom line*. Take time to figure this out. Shopping is an impulsive, rash *reaction* to a problem. What you're looking for is a solution and action that will address the problem, assuage your anger, and leave you feeling at peace.

Let's go back to Brent, the guy who works late. His wife, Marie, could decide she does not wish to live with this situation, and get a divorce. She also could decide that if Brent isn't home when she serves dinner, she'll just put his dinner in the oven and let him warm it up and serve himself. Marie could also tell Brent that, since his schedule is unpredictable, they will each have to fend for themselves at mealtimes. Further, she might begin making plans for herself in the evening rather than waiting around for Brent to come home. She could go to the movies with a friend, listen to her favorite music, work on a project. In short, she would try to detach herself emotionally from the issue of the time her husband comes home and focus instead on simply pleasing herself.

As you're reading this you might be thinking, Yeah, but her husband should come home if he cares about his marriage and his wife. It *would* be nice if Brent could get home earlier. But the demands of his job may be such that if he wants to keep it, he has to work late. Or he may be addicted to work. He also might be a perfectionist who feels uneasy leaving until all the day's work is done and he can start out with a clean desk the next morning. None of these reasons have anything to do with loving Marie or valuing their marriage. Brent is responding to his own feelings and needs about work, and trying to change him is futile. His feelings are strong and legitimate, and he is unlikely to change unless *he* becomes dissatisfied with the arrangement.

Changing Your Behavior

This leads to the hardest concept of this book: the only one you can change or control, is yourself. I hated this concept at first and railed against the injustice of it. "It's not fair," I'd moan to my shrink. "Husbands *should* do this or that; it's only equitable. Marriage is give and take, and both people have to make compromises." And on and on I went. He'd look at me dolefully and say, "But Carolyn, Gil is happy the way he is. He's happy being a couch potato, he's happy watching TV. *Your happiness is up to you.*" What????? I, like so many women, was brought up to believe that my happiness is tightly bound up in my relationships. If they were less than I wanted them to be, I was unhappy. If I was unhappy, the fault lay with the relationships and the people in them, including, of course, my husband. We had a responsibility to make each other happy and I was responsible for making him happy. If I was unhappy, he was *at least* 50 percent to blame. On other days the percentages went much higher, and I secretly felt that the creep was 98 percent to blame.

In the most general sense, my happiness *is* connected to my relationships. I can't imagine that ever changing. The difference is that now I am aware of so many different choices that I have in those relationships—ways to *make myself happy.* If my husband likes to spend a good part of the weekend days rooted to the couch, so be it. I am happiest outdoors, so I'm constructing my life so that I have plenty of opportunity to do that—without him. If he wants to join me, terrific. If not, I love what I'm doing enough to have a fine time without him. When we come together in the evening, we're both content because we've each spent the day as we wished.

In her sixth and seventh therapy sessions, Vicki and I addressed this very issue—learning to make herself happy.

Vicki: Assuming Responsibility

During her sixth therapy session, Vicki was frustrated and furious about a rather irresponsible man named Derrick who works for her husband Phil. Phil's office is in a converted house. He had given Derrick permission to move into one of the back rooms and turn it into a bedroom for himself, since he had nowhere else to stay. Vicki loathes this man and hated the idea of running into him every time she went to Phil's office. To make matters worse, Phil had invited Derrick to have Christmas dinner with them.

Vicki was outraged on two counts. First, Phil didn't ask her if it was okay to invite Derrick, and second, she did not want to eat Christmas dinner with "that man!" Despite her reaction, she knew Phil wouldn't disinvite the guy, and she felt discounted and betrayed by her husband. We discussed her alternatives and eventually got down to her bottom line. Phil could have Christmas dinner with Derrick, but she would not. She had no idea what she'd do instead.

Vicki bounced into her seventh session dressed from head to toe in pink: pink pants, pink sweater with a pink turtleneck tucked underneath. Excitedly, she recounted her weekend. When she left our last session, she said she was down and couldn't imagine how the Christmas situation would resolve itself. Then, Saturday she casually discussed Christmas with a friend. When asked what she and Phil were doing for Christmas, Vicki replied, "Phil's going out to dinner with Derrick, and I'm not sure what I'm going to do."

Her friend immediately invited her to dinner, saying that many of their mutual friends would be there as well. Vicki was delighted and utterly content to spend Christmas night with her friends while Phil took Derrick out. Bubbling, Vicki related her plans to Phil, who asked, "Was I invited, too?" "Of course," she responded. Phil didn't say anything more about the subject, but the next day he informed Vicki that he'd be going with her to their friend's home for Christmas dinner. He said he'd made other plans for Derrick. Vicki could not believe how easily this touchy situation had worked out. She was amazed to discover that when she changed herself—when she became comfortably independent—Phil's behavior changed as well. Vicki was pleased about that, but she was even more delighted with the knowledge that she had choices. She was no longer a helpless victim.

DEPRESSION

For some women, depression and a shopping fix are linked like a Pavlovian experiment. Trouble lifts its shaggy head when depression grabs hold of them, and shopping is their only response. The first step toward changing that response is understanding what's getting you down. For starters, think back over the last few days and see what experiences you've had or what unpleasant thoughts ran through your mind that may still be nagging at you.

Often the cause of transitory depression can be something as mundane as a frustrating experience with a bank teller. If it turns out that your depression is connected to an experience like that, consider the following options: first, rehearse (but don't obsess) how you could handle the situation differently next time. If you're still bothered, call the bank and, using "I" messages, tell the clerk about your feelings. Begin by saying, "I have a problem about something that happened yesterday, and I'd like to talk to you about it."

Generally, try to get rid of niggling little grievances as promptly as you can. It allows you to have a happier day and prevents these annoyances from piling up.

Pissy Little Incidents that Grow into Big Piles

Years ago, when my kids were small, the half hour I spent washing a load of dishes always seemed to be the time I would pick to get myself worked up and then depressed about some unresolved issue. It's hard to believe now, but one incident stuck in my craw for years. One night some older friends of my late husband came over to play bridge. The wife—I'll call her Mrs. X—walked into the kitchen, and one of my cats was sitting on the kitchen table. That was not unusual—our cats pretty much sat where they wanted. Anyway, she walked in and, in a peremptory way, ordered my cat off my table in my house! I was furious. Still, I could partially understand her feelings, because she was a germ freak. A lot of people don't like animals lounging on tables and countertops. But that wasn't the point; I resented her ignoring my husband's and my values in our home. In other words, it was a turf problem.

As incidents like these accumulated, I grew angrier, resentful, and depressed—depressed, because I was intimidated and had no idea how to set limits with people like Mrs. X *at the time they happened.* As the years went by, confronting her became even more difficult, because I felt that if I ever opened my mouth about some small thing, a whole torrent of rage would slosh out and drown us all. I was a living example of the quote by Lerner earlier in this chapter—I had sold out my selfhood to keep peace in a relationship.

If you are depressed, look inside yourself and notice the little and big things you're not saying. It's hard to say them, I know, but it's harder still to fully enjoy life and feel at peace when they're gnawing away at your insides.

Long-standing Depression

The frustration I just wrote about went on for years, but most of my depressed feelings were limited to the complexity of living in a stepfamily situation and dealing with Mrs. X. My rage and self-anger (depression) would surface only when I let another incident pass without standing up for myself. Otherwise, life was pretty good. But for many people, chronic, invasive depression is a way of life. It's not just a blip on an otherwise happy graph. If you have this kind of painful depression that drags on, you should get professional help. In many cases, depressed feelings can be lifted through medication in about three weeks. Then you will have the interest and energy to address what's causing your unhappiness.

Depression often comes from the same source as mine did—unexpressed anger. If we're mad at someone but fail to express it, the anger stays with us. Frequently we turn the anger against ourselves because we did not have the guts to express it out loud. So instead of staying angry with someone else, we unconsciously become angry with ourselves, our self-esteem withers, and we get depressed. Just as often it comes from an entirely different source, such as unrealistically high expectations of oneself. People with addictive personalities are often overly conscientious and perfectionistic. They wear their self-love down to a nub with their constant self-criticism. Small wonder they don't want to get up in the morning. Perfectionism will be discussed in a later section, but remember, it is a big, hulking cause of depression.

When we who have shopping problems first start to feel better, our inclination is to treat ourselves to something special and go on a bit of a spree because we've been feeling so lousy. This is called "entitlement." Before you do go shopping, it's a good idea to wait until that feeling has passed and you've been feeling good for at least a few days. Otherwise you risk a shopping bender that would lead you right back into depression.

POWERLESSNESS

Depression slithers in the same door with feelings of powerlessness. To compensate for our feelings of vulnerability and helplessness, we often turn to shopping, where we can be in charge of at least some of the transactions in our lives. Rosa, a twenty-four-year-old shopaholic and diabetic, is haunted by regrets about her past and the powerlessness she feels about her future.

Rosa

Like some married twenty-four year olds, Rosa, a diabetic, is still heavily involved with her first family. She comes from a family that is "negatively enmeshed," which means that the family members see one another constantly, but at the expense of everyone's emotional health. Rosa's father is an alcoholic, and her mother feels so depressed about her marriage that she develops "an ailment a week" to get attention. Unfortunately, her grown children furnish that attention at the expense of their own relationships. Rosa spends a hefty part of each day at her parents' home, for reasons that are quite complicated.

The situation began about five years ago, when Rosa became engaged to Mario. Her parents had heard that pregnancy could be life-threatening for diabetic women, so they got together with her doctor and pressured her into having a tubal ligation before she ever married. Only nineteen at the time, Rosa did not want the operation, but had no idea how to defend herself against the demands brought by her parents and physician. She had the operation, married, and shortly thereafter became depressed.

She also developed an obsessive-compulsive disorder that centered around her dog Muffin. Rosa became terrified that if she left Muffin alone during the day while she was at work, something terrible would happen to him, although she wasn't sure exactly what. She worried about a fire or perhaps someone breaking into her apartment, and consequently she developed elaborate rituals to make sure her dog would be okay. (I think Rosa's fears about her dog were symbolic of what had happened to her. She felt that if she were not on guard, terrible things could happen to her, and she would be powerless to do anything to prevent them.)

Before she left in the morning, she'd double check all of the windows to make sure each one was locked. Then she'd check and recheck the gas stove to make sure the burners were off. Last, she locked the front door, but she had to go back five to ten times to check it before she was reassured enough to get into her car and leave for her full-time job. Eventually, Rosa quit this job and took a part-time one near her parents' home. Rosa no longer has to worry about her dog, because she takes him over to her parents' house on the way to work and picks him up at two o'clock in the afternoon. But she doesn't just pick up Muffin and return home. Instead, she and her mother run errands and go shopping every afternoon.

Rosa would like to have children and has begun talking to specialists on her own about reversing the tubal ligation.

*But she's not planning to do anything about becoming preg-
nant quickly, because her marriage is not a happy one. It
seems that Mario spends most of each weekend hanging out
with the guys, drinking beer, and working on cars. Rosa has
asked Mario to cut down on his drinking and spend more time
with her, but to no avail. Bored and depressed, she ends up
shopping away the weekend with her mother.*

*There's more to Rosa's story that's even more depressing,
but just this much makes clear the connection between powerlessness and depression. Her parents and doctor had seized this
young woman's right to decide for herself whether she wanted
to have children. She may still be able to have children, but
it's an iffy situation over which she has little control. She feels
equally powerless about the course her diabetes will take over
her lifetime. Although she's conscientious about her diet and
shots, she can still become ill very quickly if her blood sugar
drops radically. She would like a closer relationship with her
husband but is powerless to control his behavior.*

*Rosa's life seems to be filled with powerlessness and repressed
anger. Disappointed and frustrated with her somewhat im-
mature husband, she turns to her parents for solace and
entertainment. Her behavior complements their needs nicely,
which is to distract themselves from their own unsatisfactory
marriage. Unfortunately, Rosa's dependence on her parents
makes it too threatening to face the deep anger she feels toward
them for manipulating her into having a tubal ligation.*

*Rosa says she would like to come to therapy on a regular
basis but is unable to do so because of the cost. Ironically, if she
cut down on her compulsive shopping she would have enough
money to attend therapy regularly and get to the source of her
depression.*

What to Do When You Feel Powerless

When feelings of powerlessness set in, take a look at
whether or not you're truly helpless. In my situation with
Mrs. X, with whom I played bridge, I wasn't powerless, but

rather scared. If I had decided to confront Mrs. X, I could have rehearsed what I'd say, anticipated my fear and anxiety, and steeled myself to feel nervous, but not be controlled by the feeling. Rosa's case is different. There are some things in her life that she cannot change. She is a diabetic, and her future health depends on both her own efforts and nature's unpredictable whims. The same with having children. When certain parts of our lives are completely beyond our control, like Rosa's, we have no choice but to accept them.

Giving in to our powerlessness takes considerable emotional work. First we have to come to terms with the fact that no matter how much we worry, agonize, and try to manipulate certain outcomes, it will do no good. Once we really accept that, then it's helpful to have some sense about who or what will decide those things. Some people believe in God and turn that part of their lives over to him or her. Others have faith that the universe, or karma, or *something*, will watch out for them. I've agonized about mountains of things I couldn't control and have learned that almost everything turns out okay. So I have developed a lot of faith—based on experience—in the way life treats me.

Finding a belief or conviction to help you through the many uncertain patches of life not only will be comforting, but should help you ward off depression as well. This is spirituality, which means a belief in anything nonmaterial, and it is a great help for those of us who tend to get depressed and anxious when our lives are uncertain.

DEPRIVATION AND ENTITLEMENT

It is hard to overstate the importance of deprivation and entitlement as powerful motivators in overshopping. Many of us come from homes in which we experienced emotional or financial deprivation, or both. While we don't dwell on the things we didn't get in childhood, we nonetheless are like little runaway kids. We migrate through life with thin, reedy sticks bobbing on our shoulders, tied at the end with empty red kerchiefs.

Our sense of deprivation is usually unconscious but chronic. When we feel we've done without in so many ways, either materially or emotionally, we react with an inbred sense of entitlement, of deserving more. Consciously or unconsciously, we seek compensation for our early or current deprivation. Having been brought up in families and a society that looks outward rather than inward for succor and meaning, we fill our empty sacks with externals—material things—but find they don't bring us the happiness we long for.

One of my clients has difficulty with this issue, and when she is greatly disappointed by something she can't do or buy, she looks around rather frantically for something to make herself feel better. She has yet to master the art of sitting still and letting her feelings of disappointment run their course and eventually fade away. Instead, she responds with a knee-jerk reaction. If she can't have X, then she wants to compensate herself by buying Y. But Y doesn't really appease feelings of deprivation and so she feels entitled to more and more.

During my own recovery, I pulled a classic act of entitlement, although I didn't know what I was doing. Gil and I had planned to go to Florida over the Christmas holidays but prudently decided to stay home and save money. I was tired. I'd been working very hard and fantasized about this vacation all the time. When we decided not to go, my sense of deprivation was enormous. Rather than just experience my sadness and disappointment about not going, I wanted to do something fast to take away the sting. I didn't want to feel my feelings. So I hotfooted it down to a local store and bought a four hundred–dollar suede outfit. I rationalized this by thinking to myself, Well, what the hell. We're saving three thousand bucks by not going to Florida, so we can afford this outfit. Besides, I hadn't been buying many clothes. Even Gil was amazed at how much space there was between the things hanging in my closet, and that helped me justify the outfit.

Nevertheless, I was still reacting to disappointment in the same old way.

Consequently, we need to be extremely careful about depriving ourselves. That is not to say that we get to have everything we want. Rather, it means we have to be judicious about two things: one, not setting ourselves up for something we want or need and then abandoning our plans altogether. If finances or other commitments make our plans unrealistic, we should quickly make an alternative plan that may not be as grand but won't leave us feeling deprived, either; and two, trying to keep close tabs on our feelings. When we get blue, sad, depressed, tired, or hopeless, our sense of entitlement is primed to race to the rescue. But that can get us into an even larger mess.

I have since learned that most twelve-step programs are fully aware that people with addictions are especially vulnerable at certain times. These times conveniently spell the word *Halt*, which means be aware when you are *h*ungry, *a*ngry, *l*onely, and *t*ired.

In *How to Get Out of Debt, Stay Out of Debt and Live Prosperously*, Jerrold Mundis has another, somewhat amusing list of reasons why people feel entitled to spend. Here's part of it:

- You're home all day with two young children

- You had a rotten childhood

- You stay married

- You bought everyone else presents

- You got divorced

- You were sick

- You met your deadline

- You got a raise

- You went through an awful weekend with your parents

- Your spouse doesn't understand you

- Your daughter doesn't need orthodontics after all

- Your picture was in the paper

- You've suffered a lot

- Your dog had puppies

NOTE: Reprinted by permission of Bantam Books, a division of Bantam, Doubleday, Dell Publishing Group, Inc. Copyright © 1988 by Jerrold Mundis.

This might be a good time to think about your favorite standby rationalizations. Dig a pencil out of the drawer, grab a piece of paper, and make a list, one through five.

To sum up, there's very little doubt that if we are over-shopping, we've either experienced some serious deprivation during childhood or in our lives right now. Allowing ourselves to experience the pain about what we've missed or are missing is not fun, but it is the very best way to climb out of the addiction trap. Trying to deaden our feelings is how we got to such a low point in the first place. It's only logical that the way out is to *feel*—especially the crummy stuff. *We must feel to heal.* On a cheerier note, bear in mind that when we allow ourselves to experience the misery, we also undo the padlock on our genuinely happy and joyous feelings. Many of us erroneously believe that we can just squash our negative feelings and allow ourselves to feel the happier ones. But once we begin the process of repressing or denying feelings, we also lose the power to decide which ones we'll bury and which ones we'll feel.

When you finally allow your feelings to come to the

surface, don't be terrified. The news is not going to be all bad. You will recall, and feel, many good things.

AVOIDING THE PRESENT

When we don't want to feel our current feelings, one way to avoid them is to stay focused on the past or the future: Today stinks, but when I get that new————(dress, house, baby, promotion, family room, painting, wallpaper, vacation), I'm going to feel wonderful, we tell ourselves. This is another distancing technique we latch onto to numb the pain of today. In a simplified way, it's like saying, When I have————I'll be happy. But it never works out like that. When the new car, or whatever, finally rolls into our lives, it *is* exciting, but only for a few days. Then we're back to scheming about new things to look forward to so that we can escape the present.

EMPTINESS

When we're caught up in an addictive process, it's because there are many feelings we're trying to avoid. When we repress these feelings, we feel disconnected from ourselves, our families, and anything spiritual that might fill the vacuum. In *Pathway to Recovery*, Philip Kavanaugh explains this kind of emptiness.

> There is an emptiness in all of us, a void that we constantly seek to fill. We seek to fill the void by activity, restlessness, accomplishment, by any of a thousand addictions. Spiritual teachers have always recognized this and addressed it in their writings and teachings. *This void must be "felt" not "filled" in order for us to recover."* (Italics added.)

This is how he suggests feeling the void:

One way is to sit or lie quietly, by ourselves and "tune out" our thoughts, and simply feel our feelings. This means noticing what we are experiencing within our bodies—tension, tightness, pressure, pain, sadness, fear, shakiness—whatever—and letting ourselves feel or experience these sensations *until they are gone.* What we learn from this is that if we allow ourselves to experience feelings—they will go away. No matter what the feeling is. . . . Feelings can be distressing, scary, exhausting—but they're not dangerous. *We can never be hurt by our feelings, only by the actions we take on those feelings.* The most commonly neglected area in recovery is Process—experiencing the emotions from childhood which have been buried alive.

It would almost seem, from what he's saying, that if we were to be quiet and allow ourselves to feel, and thus allow our feelings to pass, we would again be empty. But this is not so. Instead of being numb, as we were before, we are at long last able to live the moment. When we're attentive to each moment, we become acutely aware of what's around us. That's why children seem so much more alive—they're totally absorbed in their play, exploration, or feelings. In a sense that's our goal—to react in a healthy, spontaneous, and feeling way to each and every moment, perhaps a bit like children do.

If you decide to get better acquainted with your old and current feelings, I would suggest that you begin this tuning-in process slowly. Start with five minutes a day, and stick with that time for about a week. Then add five minutes more, and so on, until you're up to about half an hour. I think the idea of lying down and doing nothing for half an hour would drive most of us nuts unless we allow ourselves to get used to it slowly.

If you find that you're not feeling much, your body can give you clues. For instance, fear is felt in the stomach, thighs, legs, and feet, while anger tightens our backs, foreheads, arms, hands, jaws, and teeth. Many people feel sadness just where you'd expect it—in the center of the chest. Or they may feel tightness in the sides of the neck or in their sinuses. According to Helene Rothschild, a colleague of mine, our bodies are very literal. She offers these assessments of our bodies' tensions:

Chest: "I feel stifled, suffocated."

Eyes: "I don't want to see . . ."

Ears: "I don't want to hear . . ."

Hands: " I don't know what to do. I cannot handle it."

Knees: "I cannot stand on my own two feet."

Throat: "I am afraid to say . . ."

Genital area: "I am feeling vulnerable, so I am closing down." Or "I am afraid of my own sexuality. I am angry or hurt and so I will not let him or her in."

If your feelings stay hidden, don't be concerned; it will take them a while to reach consciousness. In the meantime, you're learning an invaluable tool—the eventual peace and tranquility that comes with stillness.

ANXIETY

Generalized anxiety is an overall sense of fearfulness or apprehension that is not necessarily related to any specific person, thing, or event. It's a nasty, energy-sapping feeling that usually plants itself right in the middle of our stomachs. Its common description is "the butterflies," but I think that's an overly complimentary analogy. Anxiety is miserable. The causes are infinite, and I am mentioning it at this point in the chapter because one of the main causes is repressed feelings. Imagine the daily battle that is being waged in our psyches between our restrained feelings shrieking, Let me out, let me out! and our warrior defense mechanisms saying, No way! We don't want to know about you! Fortunately, we're not aware of this internal battle, or we'd go crazy. But our anxiety is a clue that a battle between feelings is underway inside.

PERFECTIONISM

Our attempts to be perfect are another source of anxiety because we are constantly pushing ourselves to do what we cannot do, to be what we are not. I think we have a pretty good idea of what *perfect* means, but the dictionary's definition is telling, because it spells out exactly what we're all trying to be: "complete in all respects; without defect or omission; . . . flawless."

It's enough to gag you, right? And yet, far too many of us think we ought to be perfect. Whatever gave us this idea? It's undoubtedly an injunction we picked up from our parents and unconsciously internalized to the point that now we hold that expectation for ourselves. Marion Woodman, an expert on addictions, suggests that we quiet that critical inner voice by recognizing it, separating it from our essence, and saying, "That's not me saying that, it's my unconscious parent blathering inside my head. *I can concentrate on hearing my own voice, my own needs, my own feelings. That's when healing begins.*"

A definition of perfectionism that I like comes from another addiction writer, Anne Wilson Schaef, who says: *"The way to be perfect is to be perfectly you!"* If we are ever going to just relax and accept ourselves, paradoxically we're going to have to wage war on our relentless inner critic. One way to do that is simply to say—STOP!—when we begin yapping at ourselves about our imperfections. So many of our self-defeating thoughts and behaviors are habits. Self-criticism is yet another example.

SELF-ESTEEM

If you have been able to muffle your self-criticism, accept your imperfections, still your anxiety, embrace your emptiness, learn to live in the moment, and find healthy ways to express your needs and anger, your self-esteem is probably superb. If not, you may want to mush on and take this final internal step toward changing your shopping habits.

High self-esteem has a number of components, but perhaps the two most important are feelings of confidence and competence, both interpersonally and in your work, and simply *liking yourself*. The term self-esteem is literal, in that it means esteeming yourself. It is not connected in any way to what others may think of you or how you rate in comparison to others. To turn your self-esteem over to someone else is a precarious move, because so very often what others think of us is a projection of their own needs and values. Let's say, for instance, that you meet a woman at a luncheon. You're drawn to her right away but sense that she is cool toward you. Is that because something is wrong with you, or is it a result of some conscious or unconscious feeling within her? Perhaps just the way you tilt your head when you talk reminds her of a hated aunt. Or she feels intimidated by the size of your engagement ring. In both cases, the other person's response to you comes from inside her and has nothing to do with who you are.

If you don't turn over your self-esteem to someone else, then it will reside in your (perhaps) not-too-gentle hands. I'm implying that if you are a perfectionist and accept nothing but the best, you may not be very kind to yourself. I would suggest then, that you begin using the same yardstick on yourself that you use on your friends. We know our friends' faults and shortcomings, but we like them anyway. Why should it be any different with ourselves? Why do we subject ourselves to far harsher scrutiny? It doesn't make sense. In fact, sometimes our friends' faults are a bit of a relief. They allow us to be human, too.

For example, one time I had a client who was an image

consultant. Every week she came in looking absolutely perfect. Her hair, her makeup, her clothes, her accessories, her posture, and even her fingernails were flawless. It was awful. I felt like a bag lady and had a terrible time relaxing. Her perfectionism also made it hard for me to trust her. If she had such high standards for herself, what kind of miracles would she expect from me? So if you, like me, are less than perfect, *embrace your ordinariness*. It allows you to be friends with yourself and others.

How Parental Messages Affect Self-Esteem

The impact of our parents' beliefs about us cannot be overstated. Many people spend their entire lives trying to beat down their parents' negative evaluations and trying to replace them with ones that are more congruent with who they've become. In a recent interview, Audrey Hepburn offered some candid comments about her self-esteem that were highly revealing. As usual, I assumed that such a beautiful, talented woman would have a solid core of self-worth. Instead, her mother's belief that Audrey had no talent and her father's abandonment (the most lethal nonverbal message possible) left Audrey as frail internally as she appears externally. Now in her sixties, she summed up her feelings about herself. "I still feel I could lose everything at any moment [a consequence of her father's abandonment plus the trauma of living in Europe during World War II]. But the greatest victory has been to be able to live with myself, to accept my shortcomings and those of others. I'm a long way from being the human being I'd like to be [says the dedicated philanthropist]. But I've decided I'm not so bad after all!"

If we don't want to be held hostage by our parents' deliberate or inadvertent assessments, we first have to reacquaint ourselves with their viewpoint. Many of our parents' remarks we can repeat verbatim, while others we long ago repressed. I think it's important to recall the positive and supportive things they've said as well as the negative.

To bring this material into full consciousness, I'd suggest that you get a few pieces of paper and draw a line down the middle. On the left side, write down every positive statement or belief you received from your parents (or from other important adults in your childhood). On the right side, list any negative things you can remember.

How does your list look? Is it packed with negatives and just a few positives? Or is it balanced or leaning toward positive?

If you have an entire list of negatives, it's important to confront these criticisms with the reality of who you are today. Instead of letting negative evaluations sour your self-esteem, it's time for these ancient criticisms to try to prove their case.

Take each criticism from your list and give it an honest hearing. Those that are *not* true of you today, scratch out with a big, fat pen stroke. Those that are occasionally true, give a percentage rating for accuracy. If any of your parents' views are still true, circle them. Of those that are circled, next decide how *you* feel about them. For example, do you care if you're messy or does it fit with your priorities in life? Spend time on each circled item on your list. If your parents' view of you is valid, and it's something *you* would like to change, then give it an asterisk. Since life is an ongoing process of growth and refining, take your adult assessment of a childhood criticism and use it to *challenge* not *diminish* yourself.

Next, rephrase your old self-criticism. Before you might have said something to yourself like, I'm such a slob. Now phrase this short-coming in a positive way—I would like to be neater—and let it go at that. No self-condemnation, no promises, no due dates to change, no conditional self-love. Just a simple statement of fact about yourself. Once you've banished false criticisms and others you don't care about, you should be left with a fairly short list of parental messages that *you've decided* are valid.

Take your little list, fold it up, stick it into a drawer, and, as you slowly close the drawer, think to yourself, Yup, those shortcomings are a part of me. Ignore the list, work on it—

whatever you choose—but, above all else, remember that your list of faults admits you to the world of flawed people. Everyone's there, so don't feel reluctant to join us.

In this chapter we've looked at some of the underlying feelings and beliefs that lead you to splurge. In the next chapter you'll find practical tips, suggestions, and plans to help you bring your shopping and spending into balance.

Chapter 10

Balanced Shopping: A Step-by-Step Program

The goal of both this chapter and the book is to help you master your shopping. *This does not mean abstinence.* This last sentence is emphasized for two reasons. First, unless we take the veil and disappear into a cloister, shopping is a necessary part of our everyday lives. We can't quit altogether. Second, never again getting to shop for fun immediately conjures up feelings of panic and deprivation. Any sense of deprivation will, in turn, paradoxically hinder the goal of bringing our shopping under control. It was our feelings of deprivation that caused our excesses in the first place. More deprivation will only make the problem worse. So rather than heading toward abstinence, we will be working toward balance. Balance in our lives, balance in our shopping.

We cannot handle our external life with steadiness unless our internal life is harmonious; consequently, the first eight steps of the following eleven-step balanced shopping program, will continue to focus on our internal lives. The last two steps will target specific behavioral changes you can make to curtail your shopping.

STEP ONE: ACKNOWLEDGE THE PROBLEM

We've all heard the business about how you can't fix a problem until you admit you have one. That sounds crisp and logical when we're talking about *someone else*. It becomes far more disconcerting and scary when we are talking about ourselves, and the fact that *we* may be the ones with the problem. Who wants to confront shortcomings in themselves? I certainly didn't. I'd flutter around my problem, one day thinking, Well, I'm just a shopaholic, that's not such a bad deal. Other times I'd look at my very affluent friends' shopping behavior and think, Pooh, I don't have a problem at all. Then there were the darker days, when I'd admit to myself that my spending was getting (notice the tempering—*getting*) out of hand.

Problems like ours are simply symptoms—symptoms that something is awry in our lives. In the realm of physical health, we carefully note any signs of trouble, because we've learned that attending to our symptoms is a positive thing to do. If our thoats are scratchy, we may up our vitamin C intake, pop some zinc, get a throat culture, or simply take it easy for a few days. We notice physical symptoms and take preventive measures because we don't want to get sicker. In some instances we go a step further—we look for signs of trouble even when we don't have any symptoms. We regularly endure the indignity of having a Pap smear, allowing our doctors to scrape our cervixes for signs of possible trouble. Then our potential for trouble is given a number: "one" means we're in the clear, "two or three" bear watching, and "four" is ominous.

But with emotional problems, we're far more reluctant to admit *to ourselves,* I've got a problem. That stems from our negative biases about emotional ill health. Somehow it's okay for our bodies to develop problems but it's not okay for our souls. Physical disease is upsetting but acceptable; emotional *dis-ease* is upsetting and shameful. The irony is that emotional symptoms, such as overshopping, are not necessarily harbingers of a serious illness, but rather tickles that invite us to appraise our lives and make some readjustments so we'll be happier.

If you've been too scared to take the quizzes in chapter 3, go ahead and do so now. Whatever you learn about yourself won't be fatal, so there's no reason to panic. If it should turn out that you are addicted, somewhere inside yourself you already knew that anyway. So the quiz just confirms the accuracy of your own self-perceptions.

STEP TWO: GET SUPPORT AND HELP

Ordinarily in self-help books and programs, getting outside help is usually the *last* solution if you can't fix things by yourself. I don't agree with this. If you can find a twelve-step group in your area, I would encourage you to join now, while you're just starting to work on your shopping or spending problem. Twelve-step groups work with addiction. The original group, Alcoholics Anonymous (AA), was formed to help alcoholics become sober. Because of AA's success, mental health workers have come to the conclusion that the most effective program for any addiction—chemical or process—is a twelve-step program. Addicted shoppers and spenders have their own twelve-step program called Debtors Anonymous. Since our problems have just been recognized, as opposed to those of alcoholics, there aren't a lot of DA groups around. But there are some in almost all large cities, and the phone numbers can generally be found in the white pages under Debtors Anonymous. If you don't find a group listed, you can write to: Debtors Anonymous, General Services Board, P.O. Box 20322, New York, NY 10025-9992.

If there isn't a DA group meeting nearby, then there are a number of other groups you can attend that will offer great support and wisdom, even though they may be talking about other addictions. For instance, Overeaters Anonymous (OA) and Gamblers Anonymous are two other groups that deal with process addictions. Substance abuse programs will work, too, as well as Al-Anon, Adult Children of Dysfunctional Families or Adult Children of Alcoholics (ACA) groups. The chief reason that any, or all, of these groups work so well is that the program in each group is basically the same. If you go to an OA meeting, for instance, people will be talking about their struggles to respond in healthy ways to the stresses in their lives—rather than raid the refrigerator.

They raid refrigerators, we raid stores. It's almost the same. So you just substitute the word *debtor* for *overeater* in your mind, and the help will be the same. I've been to OA and Al-Anon and found their meetings practically identical to DA. One of the things I love about these meetings is that people check their camouflages and egos at the door; they are bare-boned honest about themselves, and no one tries to impress anyone about anything. You have no idea what people do for a living, how much money they make, what kind of cars they drive, or any of the other stuff that ordinarily helps us define and promote ourselves to others. The people are about as pretentious as TV's Roseanne.

Debtors Anonymous

Here's how the meetings work that I've attended. People straggle in, grab a cup of coffee, say hello to people they know (most people are friendly), and sit down, and the meeting starts. Someone will read a short statement about addiction. Another person will be the official speaker for that particular meeting, and he or she will talk about his or her struggle with debting, what they've gotten out of the program, and where they are now in their recovery process.

Then others in the meeting voluntarily talk about a problem or success they've had in the past week or two. Since the meetings last only an hour to an hour and a half, just a few people have time to speak, and then it's time to quit. The meeting ends with the Lord's Prayer. Since people do not respond to one another's stories except to say thank you, there's no direct advice given about how to solve problems. The help comes in three ways: through listening to others' struggles and successes, from working with a twelve-step program, and from pressure groups and pressure meetings, which are designed to help take the pressure *off* people financially.

Pressure Groups and Pressure Meetings

Pressure groups meet at the request of a member to help her take the pressure off herself. A pressure group would consist of a woman and a man from the DA group who are in recovery, plus yourself. Your spouse would be encouraged to come as well, so that he could participate in the discussion and planning. From this meeting, which typically lasts about two hours, an assessment would be made of your financial picture. That assessment would include what you need for survival. Then items that are crucial to your happiness would be included—things like a health club membership, flowers, hobby equipment, and so on. These personal needs, or wants, are considered pivotal because of the understanding that "we in Debtors Anonymous are committed to repaying our debts in full, but we have found by bitter experience that we will never be able to accomplish that task unless we first take care of ourselves." At this meeting or a subsequent meeting, a debt repayment plan would be devised, and you would begin to contact your creditors and inform them of your repayment plans. DA does not encourage or endorse bankruptcy as a solution to indebtedness.

New members are encouraged to get a sponsor. Sponsors are people who have been in the program a while and are making progress with their own spending, shopping, or debting. The sponsor is the person you're encouraged to turn to with your problems.

Why not wait and see if you can beat your shopping problems on your own? Because the knowledge, support, understanding, and humor that are to be found in DA meetings will speed your recovery. They also will keep you honest with yourself and build your self-esteem. By the way, the meetings are free, although they do pass a basket and almost everyone throws in a dollar or two (the first meeting is on the house). If you feel too embarrassed to go, and thereby admit that you have a problem, remember that everyone else there has exactly the same problem. Often they've got it even worse. Nonetheless, if you're not ready to do this now, that's fine. Maybe later. Or maybe never. You know what's best for you.

Counselors and therapists can also be a terrific source of insight and support as you begin changing your shopping patterns. They are especially good at helping you piece together why you have your problem as well as helping when you overcome stumbling blocks during your recovery. I deliberately didn't say *if* you run into stumbling blocks, because setbacks are something you can count on.

STEP THREE: DEFINE WHAT YOU WANT TO CHANGE

It's not possible for us to recover from anything until we know exactly what we mean by *recover*. If we are sick with the flu, we call work and let them know we won't be in until we feel well enough to work. That's our definition of recovery, and we use that yardstick to help us figure out if we're up to going back to the office. If we're still dizzy and have a temperature, we say, Forget it! and go back to bed. We haven't reached our own definition of recovery. Getting precise about our recovery from excessive shopping is a little more difficult, because our problem is emotional and highly complex. Nonetheless, we have to do it. Otherwise we won't know what our goal is, how to get there, or when we've reached it. As Earnie Larsen put it in *Stage II Recovery,* "It's like going to a travel agency and asking for a ticket, 'Away from here!' " To help you decide where "there" might be for you, here are some of the goals I'm working on for myself:

1. To avoid dipping into our savings for any expenses except those, such as investments, that will increase our savings. Exception: my daughter's wedding and maybe a trip to Europe.

2. To avoid spending money impulsively in order to alter an uncomfortable mood.

3. To avoid going in debt.

4. To make sure that the distribution of discretionary money in our family is fair.

5. To save money regularly.

Take time now to list your goals. If it's hard to get clear exactly what they are, take as much time as you need to think it through. Here are some suggestions. If you are a shopaholic who shops excessively when you're angry at your mate, your first goal would be to cease shopping when you're angry. If you're an addicted shopper who shops when something sets off your deprivation alarm, your goal would be to avoid shopping during those times. We'll get to the mechanics of reaching these goals a little later. When you're clear about what your goals are, get a piece of paper and write them down, one through five.

Given your definition of your problem, it's now time to think in a general sense about what triggers it. If you shop when you're mad at your husband, your goal might be to figure out what kinds of things you're getting angry about and to decide whether there's a pattern to them. If deprivation sends you hurtling out to the mall, try to become aware of the kinds of deprivation that you react to. Are you vulnerable when you've been working too hard and need to nurture yourself? Or does it hit when your mother calls and nags at you for the millionth time?

Last, given your definition of your problem, where will

your program of recovery take you? The shopaholic may decide to look closely at the areas of contention in her marriage and seek help getting them resolved. Or she may see that the sources of her anger will never change and decide to leave her marriage. Of course, the ultimate destination of recovery will be to cease excessive shopping.

STEP FOUR: TRACE THE ORIGINS OF YOUR PROBLEM

As you read in chapter 4, the roots of our addictions stem from our early family interactions. Even though most of our stresses may be current, our families taught us how to react to feelings, stress, and people. If we consciously understand how they readied us for life, then we'll understand why we respond to circumstances as we do. Now is the time to revisit your childhood with honesty, trying not to deny what you felt. As a child you probably had to deny to survive. But that's no longer true. Now your memories and feelings may be painful, but they aren't unsafe. As mentioned before, repressing our childhood feelings causes far more damage than inviting them into consciousness. Once you allow yourself to feel your experiences with emotion, you can move on. Otherwise, repressed feelings tend to recur in destructive repetitions and without resolution.

Jennifer has been struggling with her father's rejection throughout her whole adult life, and she reacts to men in her adult life as if they were her father.

Jennifer

Jennifer, who was introduced in chapter 4, reacts irrationally, almost violently, when a boyfriend or a woman friend chooses to spend time with a female other than herself. She feels jealous, betrayed, and enraged. She wants to end the relationship that very minute. In her fury, she's done just that many times and then has felt great sadness afterward. At the same time she also feels safe, because the person who slighted her can never hurt her again.

The origin of Jennifer's overreaction lies in her relationship with her father. Although he left the family when Jennifer was six, he showed up on weekends to see the kids—except that he didn't see all of the kids. He'd ignore Jennifer and her younger brother, but take Jennifer's younger sister, whom he'd take to the movies, buy presents, and otherwise dote over. Had her father chosen to spend time with his son, Jennifer's pain might have been a little less, because of the natural bond between fathers and sons. But instead he chose her cute little sister. Why he behaved in this manner is a puzzle to Jennifer.

Although Jenny had therapy before, she hadn't spent much time talking about her relationship with her father. She's just now beginning to see why she becomes hysterical when a friend appears to choose another female over her. Although it is painful for her to go back and remember the hurt she felt as a child, she needs to understand and grieve for the little girl in her that received such insensitive treatment. Otherwise, she's going to continue to act out her little girl pain in her current life and have a lot of difficulty with friendships and love relationships.

Just recently Jennifer fell in love with a divorced man, Simon, who has two little daughters from his previous marriage. This man's family constellation is especially painful for Jennifer, because she perceives his daughters as a threat to the love Simon has for her. Consequently, she struggles with this issue of underlying trust every day. At the same time Jennifer is beginning to believe that this man loves her for who she is. Not for her beauty, not for her body, and not for her extravagant wardrobe.

When looking at your childhood, consider the following core issues to see how they've affected you. You may want to spend some time thinking about each question and writing down your responses.

1. Fear of abandonment: was your parents' love (and presence) secure and steady or unreliable?

2. Was your parents' love for you unconditional, or did it depend on any number of variables, many of which you couldn't understand, much less meet at the time?

3. Predictability: was your parents' behavior reliable and appropriate, or was it chancy, threatening, or embarrassing?

4. Shame: were your physical, emotional, and spiritual needs respected, or were they violated, leaving you with a feeling of shame about yourself?

5. Did your family stress the importance of honoring one's own beliefs, needs, and wishes, or was the emphasis on external approval—what would be acceptable to others?

6. Were you encouraged to deaden your emotional responses and behave like little adults?

7. Were certain thoughts, feelings, and emotions taboo? Were you encouraged to not even think about certain things because they were shameful, much less discuss them?

8. Were your parents perfectionists? Did they expect perfection from you?

9. Were your parents intrusive? Did they blur the boundaries between your individuality and privacy and their right to know every little thing about you?

STEP FIVE: ASSESS YOUR NEEDS

Although women tend to equate happiness and satisfaction with the condition of their relationships, step five sets aside those relationships and puts *you* on center stage. Pretend for a few chilling moments that you don't have a husband, lover, kids, or friends. What would your life be like? Do you have work (salaried or volunteer) that is stimulating and satisfying? Or do your days loom long and boring, with duties and activities that simply fill the time?

If you have strong needs for stimulation, are you meeting them in direct, healthy ways or through self-destructive dramas? If you are charged up and energetic by nature, what are you doing with your vitality? Are you burning up your abundance in frenetic shopping, or have you found more direct, physical outlets? Are you doing justice to your creativity? It's an enormous gift, but one that is easy to discount because it is not highly valued in our culture. Is it time to take a risk with your creativity and find another job that will allow you to use your talents? If you dabble in the arts, do you want to invest more of your time developing your skills by taking classes? Would you be happier if you found friends who share your interests?

STEP SIX: DISCOVER WHAT REALLY MAKES YOU HAPPY

In this step the focus remains on you. When we're caught up in a shopping spree, there's a part of us that feels excited. But it's not a lasting feeling; it turns on us and eventually we feel lousy. However, one of the biggest obstacles to giving up this particular fix or addiction is not believing that *anything that gives us the same lift* can take its place. So before you consider quitting, I think it's imperative that you've already begun adding activities to your life that bring you as much or more pleasure than shopping. That way you avoid throwing yourself into a deprivation crisis.

A good place to start is with your childhood. The kinds of activities that brought us great joy as children are likely to still have appeal in their adult forms. The other evening my husband and I were in a bookstore. Ordinarily Gil isn't particularly tempted by books. But this time, he drifted off somewhere, and a few minutes later he came back with an enormous, fat book clutched to his chest. His eyes danced and he had a delighted, yet sheepish, look on his face that I'd never seen before. Somewhat like a little boy, he extended his book and said, "I'm gonna buy this book!" What was it? A book full of beautiful pictures of airplanes, replete with fine detail and exquisite color. The book was on sale for forty dollars, but even two hundred dollars would have been cheap just to see his joy. It turned out that when he was a boy, Gil spent hundreds of hours poring over pictures of airplanes. It's that kind of response that you may be able to recapture from your childhood and reintegrate into your adult life.

For starters, were you a child who loved the outdoors? If so, what did you like to do? Did you enjoy taking risks, doing daring, adventurous things? Or were you a child who liked the outdoors but preferred to stick closer to home or your school grounds? Did you like sports? If so, did you like the rough, contact sports? Or did you prefer those that were less competitive or combative? Did you love a pet dearly to compensate for your solitude?

If you preferred the indoors, did you like to play alone or with others? Did you like board games that challenged you, like checkers or chess, or did you prefer more passive and solitary activities, like reading, word games, sewing, or playing with dolls? Were there things you always wanted to do as a child, but for one reason or another couldn't do? Did you long to play the piano, or pirouette in a tutu, or play baseball when the boys wouldn't let you? Many of our unfulfilled childhood wishes and fantasies are available to us now. All we have to do is take a chance, put on our tap-dance shoes, and go for it.

As adults we are exposed to many activities that look appealing but, for one reason or another, we talk ourselves out of trying. Is there anything you've secretly been dying to do but have held back? Now, absolutely and positively, is the time to try any and all things that look enticing. If you scored high on the need for excitement tests in chapter 5, consider trying activities that thrill or challenge you.

Take a minute now and write down the things you currently enjoy, everything you've done in the past and loved, and anything you've every thought you might like to try. Make a plan to tackle each one of them over the next year. There's no rush, but, on the other hand, what a terrible waste not to taste everything on life's table. We've already checked out the table cloth, the crystal, the silver, and the china and found they don't do much for us. But, it's going to be hard to give up their cold glitter until we find the warm, lush joy of activities that enhance our lives.

STEP SEVEN: ASSESS YOUR RELATIONSHIPS

If you want to alter your shopping patterns, it's essential that you take a close look at your relationships. As we've seen throughout this book, our excesses are often a symptom of a relationship problem, and we cannot fix ourselves until we establish healthy relationships.

What is a healthy relationship? That, of course, depends so much on the needs of the people involved, but I think Janet Woititz's definition is as good as can be found. She says, in her book *Struggle for Intimacy,* that "you know you are in a healthy, intimate relationship when you have created an environment where:

1. I can be me.
2. You can be you.
3. We can be us.
4. I can grow.
5. You can grow.
6. We can grow together."

NOTE: Reprinted with permission of the publisher, Health Communications, Inc., from *Struggle for Intimacy* by Janet Woititz, Ed. D. Copyright © 1985.

Sometimes, though, it's hard to look honestly at important relationships. At the risk of sounding preachy, I want to
assure you that if you have the pluck to face the truth of your
relationships, in time you'll find the skills to enhance them or
the guts to give them up. To assist you, I'd like to recommend
books that my clients and I have found invaluable. They
address our relationships with ourselves and with others:

*The Agony of It All: The Drive for Drama and Excite-
ment in Women's Lives,* by Joy Davidson, Ph.D.

Love Is Letting Go of Fear, by Gerald Jampolsky, M.D.

Good-bye to Guilt: Releasing Fear Through Forgiveness,
by Gerald Jampolsky, M.D.

Stage II Recovery: Life Beyond Addiction, by Earnie
Larsen

*In Sickness and in Health: The Co-Dependent Mar-
riage,* by Mary S. Stuart

Let Go and Grow: Recovery for Adult Children, by
Robert Ackerman

Co-Dependent No More, by Melody Beattie

Learning to Love Yourself: Finding Your Self-Worth, by
Sharon Wegscheider-Cruse

*Learning to Live in the Now: 6-Week Personal Plan to
Recovery,* by Ruth Fishel

Healing the Shame that Binds You, by John Bradshaw

Bradshaw on the Family, by John Bradshaw

The Assertive Woman, by Stanlee Phelps and Nancy
Austin

Women Who Love Too Much, by Robin Norwood

How to Raise Your Self-Esteem: The Proven, Action-Oriented Approach to Greater Self-Respect and Self Confidence, by Nathaniel Branden

Love and Addiction: The First and Most Important Book on Addiction to Love, by Stanton Peele

The Dance of Anger: A Women's Guide to Changing the Patterns of Intimate Relationships, by Harriet Lerner, Ph.D.

The Dance of Intimacy: A Woman's Guide to Courageous Acts of Change in Key Relationships, by Harriet Lerner, Ph.D.

Healing the Child Within: Discovery and Recovery for Adult Children of Dysfunctional Families, by Charles Whitfield, M.D.

Struggle for Intimacy, by Janet G. Woititz, Ed.D.

The Language of Love: A Powerful Way to Maximize Insight, Intimacy, and Understanding, by Gary Smalley and John Trent, Ph.D.

Forgive and Forget: Healing the Hurts We Don't Deserve, by Lewis B. Smedes

Prospering Woman: A Complete Guide to Achieving the True, Abundant Life, by Ruth Ross, Ph.D.

STEP EIGHT: USE YOUR CREATIVITY

I am convinced that many of us who shop and spend too much do so partly because it is a form of self-expression and creativity. Many of us are right-brain dominant, highly visual, and talented. Yet, few of us have occupations that allow us to unleash our creativity. If you have secretly longed for a job that would tap your creativity, seriously consider changing occupations. I'm aware that such positions are not necessarily easy to find, but if you persist, you probably will find one.

Will it pay you as much as you're making now? Perhaps not. However, if you're happy creating, you're not going to need to blow so much money on shopping. In time the quality of your life will become paramount, and life-style sacrifices will seem worth it in order to do what you enjoy.

If you are not in a position to make a career change, then honor your creativity by devoting as much time and money to it as you can afford. Make it a priority in your spare time. Take classes that sound delicious, not practical. Try to find others who share your passion, and spend time with them. You'll discover an instant rapport with those who share your interests, and perhaps you'll develop some satisfying friendships.

If you're not sure how creative you are, take a look at two things. First, what are your hobbies and interests? If they involve some form of creative or performing arts, then you've got a creative bent. As an example, notice how you and others approach taking photographs. Most people are satisfied just to click off a roll of film lickety-split, while others savor getting just the right camera setting, background, light, and angle. I would guess that you're the latter type—the kind who wants to make something ordinary as pretty or interesting as possible.

Second, look at the occupations and hobbies of your parents, grandparents, aunts, and uncles. What did they do for work and in their leisure time? Much of our native talent is inherited rather than learned. That's why your genes can tell you a great deal about what might bring you more satisfaction than what you're presently doing. For example, was your father a great amateur photographer, and do you also yearn to take pictures? Try to live your life where your heart, not your head, takes you.

STEP NINE: IDENTIFY YOUR SHOPPING PATTERNS

An urge to splurge is usually preceded by a feeling or an event. If we chart those occurrences over time, a pattern will emerge. Once we know our pattern, we'll know when we're vulnerable and can take steps to do something different. I would suggest charting this information in a little record keeper or diary that is dated. That way you can not only have a record of your feelings but also note any patterns that have to do with the days of the month, such as premenstrual syndrome or holidays. Some people have what is called an anniversary depression, which means they get depressed on the anniversary of some unhappy event in their lives. Or you may discover that Mondays are consistently a down day for you, or that your downs follow the lunar calendar or a plunge in barometric pressure.

Your diary should be small enough to fit inside a pocket or purse, so that you can keep it with you at all times. That way, if you get an impulse to buy something unplanned, say when you're out doing errands, you can jot down whatever you're feeling before you head into the store. After you've kept your diary for a couple of months, see if there are any consistent patterns between your moods (or feelings), events, dates, and shopping. If you find any correlations, you've taken a pivotal step toward understanding your behavior and changing it. A typical page in your notebook might look like this:

Monday, March 6: Little tired, bored, boss is cranky. Lunch with Sue, $7.48.

Tuesday, March 7: Got my review; it was excellent. Went shopping after work to celebrate. Bought new suit, $185.00.

Wednesday, March 8: Feel great, wore new suit, got lots of compliments.

Thursday, March 9: Josh is going to need braces. Depressed. Went marketing, spotted this darling pair of sandals in shoe store. Decided I might as well buy them now, since things are going to get tight due to braces.

Friday, March 10: Tired, feel like a shopping hit to pick me up, but don't go.

222   How to Quit

Saturday, March 11: The Schultzes coming for dinner, afraid the table will look blah. Buy new dried flower arrangement, $42.00.

Sunday, March 12: Good day with the kids, not so good with Tom. He spends the whole day tinkering with that damn car. Thinking about the sales I saw in the Sunday supplement. Maybe I'll dash over tomorrow during lunch.

STEP TEN: EXPERIENCE NEW ALTERNATIVES

Now that you've identified the feelings that you're trying to fix with shopping, it's time to handle those feelings in a different way. A very important first step is to get comfortable with doing nothing. Well, actually, you will be doing something, which is to experience your feelings in their entirety. If you're sad, for example, that means just sitting still or lying down and letting your feelings wash over you. If you feel like crying, do so. It's very cleansing. If you're feeling anxious or jumpy, I would suggest listening to a relaxation tape, which can be bought at many bookstores and record stores. These tapes talk you through a process where you systematically tighten and relax all of the major muscle groups in your body. There's peaceful music playing in the background, and it's not uncommon to get so relaxed that you fall asleep. The relaxation experience takes about twenty to thirty minutes, and you feel wonderful afterward. By training yourself to experience feelings and to relax, you're severing the connection between uncomfortable feelings and impulsive behavior. In time you'll find you actually enjoy your new responses and won't feel deprived just because you haven't gone shopping.

By this time you've also begun integrating new activities into your life. They, too, can be your shopping substitutes. If you have found new activities that you really love, you will probably find that given the choice between shopping and your new interests, you'll choose the latter.

STEP ELEVEN: AVOID DEBTING—A NEW APPROACH TO YOUR FINANCES

The following material is taken from a book that I strongly suggest you buy called *How to Get Out of Debt, Stay Out of Debt and Live Prosperously*. The author is Jerrold Mundis, and the list price is $17.95. The book is undoubtedly available in libraries, but I suggest that you buy it so you can read it again and again. The two main points that I want to emphasize are as follows: first, the only way to get out of debt is to stop debting, which means that *each day, a day at a time, your goal is to incur no new debt*. That, in turn, means getting rid of your credit cards, so you won't be tempted to use them. Depending on the extent of your debt and your charging habits, that recommendation can be modified slightly. If you have a credit card that must be paid off every month, such as American Express and some gas cards, I think it's okay to hang on to them. Any cards that offer revolving credit plans, however, should be destroyed immediately.

Each time you use one of your one-month-pay-off cards, Mundis suggests that you immediately sit down and write a check for whatever purchase you made. That way, when the bill rolls in, you will have set aside the money to pay the charges. For security reasons, I've hung on to my American Express card and gas cards. My husband doesn't want to close any of our other charge accounts, so I've just given my cards to him. However, as we saw in chapter 2, it's all too easy to charge stuff even when you don't have the card with you. If I begin doing that, I'm going to have to insist that the accounts be closed so I can continue to recover. My husband will complain and be inconvenienced, but I think we will both benefit in the long run if such a plan becomes necessary. It's realistic to be prepared for some flack from your spouse if you decide to try this program. They certainly are entitled to their feelings, but I think your gaining control over your shopping is paramount. So don't feel guilty. You're trying to recover, and there's nothing more important than that.

The second part of Mundis's plan involves budgeting, though not budgeting in the usual way. Ordinarily, when people are establishing a budget, they list all of their fixed expenses first—all of their musts—and then allocate any left-over money for pleasure and entertainment. Mundis suggests going about it differently. First on your list are items such as food, housing, and transportation expenses. Next, a reasonable amount of money is incorporated into the budget for pleasure. Pleasure comes second, because it was our sense of deprivation and lack of satisfying activities that got most of us into debt in the first place. So to do without is self-defeating. Third, some amount is devoted to savings, and last, a repayment plan for all debts is scheduled. For many people, their debts far exceed their income, so the amount of repayment on debts will be less than the expected minimum. To get creditors off your back, Mundis suggests that you contact each one and tell them your plans for repayment. Do not wait for them to start bugging you; seize control of the situation by contacting them first, expressing your concern about your debt and your sincere dedication to repaying it.

In order to make a realistic budget, it's necessary to figure out how you're spending your money. That's where the pocket diary mentioned in step nine comes in. If you faithfully record your every purchase, you'll soon get an accurate picture of how you spend your money. That will be a great help in planning a realistic budget for the future. Mundis sums up the benefits of his program this way, "As you refrain from debting one day at a time, as you begin to prosper and liquidate your debts, you cannot fail to gain a true confidence in yourself and a genuine self-worth."

SUGGESTIONS FROM WOMEN WHO SHOP TOO MUCH

The following suggestions come from my clients and me. They're not presented in any particular order, but I think you'll find them helpful. Since you're going to continue

shopping—although hopefully less often—the first suggestions have to do with shopping sensibly.

1. Several years ago, a wardrobe consultant came
    over to my house, pawed through my closets,
    and gave me excellent advice about how to shop
    more wisely. It turned out that my clothes
    didn't fit my life-style. I had all sorts of dressy
    outfits that I never wore. I loved those kinds of
    clothes, but they didn't reflect my casual life-
    style. I was wasting a lot of money on things I
    rarely wore. She charged about eighty dollars
    for her advice, and it was well worth it.

2. I also had my colors analyzed about five years
    ago, and I've saved a bundle by doing so. Be-
    fore, I would buy whatever I was attracted to,
    without regard to how becoming it was with
    my coloring, and many of those outfits would
    hang in my closet unworn. I've since discovered
    that I feel happier and more attractive in colors
    that suit me. The clothes also mix and match
    well, which is another savings. The cost for the
    color analysis at that time was about fifty dol-
    lars.

3. I've now developed what I call the "Wesson
    Wear Average" for my clothes. This average tells
    me in the most general sense what it costs me
    to wear a given outfit every time I put it on. For
    instance, the dress I got for my wedding to Gil
    is a Diane Fries, and it cost four hundred dol-
    lars. It's not all that dressy, so it's certainly
    something I could wear to a bunch of places,
    but for some reason I don't. I've worn it maybe
    four times in four years, so that means the darn
    thing has cost me a hundred bucks per wearing.
    A tad expensive, wouldn't you say? On the other

hand, I bought a wild-looking but sensuously comfy Max sweatshirt for sixty-six dollars. It's reversible, and I imagine I've had it on at least forty times since I bought it five months ago. So that has cost me $1.65 each time I've worn it. Since I'll probably wear it like mad next winter, the cost per wear should get down to less than a dollar. But even then, it's a little surprising how much it costs to wear even those things we use a lot.

4. Another trick I've used once or twice to talk myself out of something expensive is to correlate the cost of the outfit with the price of a plane ticket. For the price of an expensive dress, for instance, I could buy a round-trip ticket to New York City or Hawaii. That usually slows me down. You can do the same thing by substituting the cost of one of your hobbies or financial goals.

5. If you're in a store and you see something you love, you might as well try it on. If you don't, it will drive you crazy wondering how it would have looked. You'll probably obsess about it and feel deprived. If you try it on, you might discover that it looks terrible and you can put the item out of your mind.

6. In AA they use the term *slippery places* to refer to bars, restaurants, or any place the alcoholic will run into booze and be tempted to drink. We have slippery places, too. For some it's a flea market, for others it's a shoe store. For many of us it's clothing stores. The very best way to avoid temptation is to avoid your slippery place.

7. Plan rewards for not going to your particular slippery place. The best kind of reward is some-

thing spiritual. By spiritual I mean anything nonmaterial. An example of a spiritual reward would be taking a drive in the countryside or a trip to the zoo. Anything that brings you joy, satisfaction, or peace is a spiritual experience. Nonspiritual rewards are terrific, too. Renting a good video, eating a chocolate ice-cream cone—anything that helps you celebrate your not shopping that day is what you're looking for.

8. One way to avoid a slippery place is to ask a friend, child, or spouse to go there for you. Let's say you need a special brand of film for your camera, and it is only carried at a camera store that's full of tempting things. Ask a friend to pick up the film for you. People love to be helpful, especially to someone who's trying to break a bad habit or fight an addiction. Helping makes them feel good about themselves, so don't be afraid to ask. Last Christmas I didn't want to go near the stores, so I asked my grown daughter to do some of it for me. She loved it. She loved choosing gifts for family members that were within my budget, which is a little larger than hers.

9. When you do decide to shop, it's a good idea to shop alone. Friends have a way of encouraging each other and helping each other rationalize purchases.

10. If you go shopping, take a list and buy only the things on that list. Plan a nonspending reward for sticking to your list.

11. Avoid sales unless you have the self-discipline to buy only those things that are on sale and that you need. Many people impulsively buy things that are on sale just because they're cheaper, but

they have no real use for the item, so their money is wasted.

12. Experiment with looking average for one week. If you're hooked on clothes this sounds like a killer, but you'll be surprised by the results. By *average* I mean dressing in a way that seems rather nondescript and non–attention getting. Drag out all of those clothes from the back of your closet that you think are boring, and wear them. When I tried this I learned all sorts of things. First, no one noticed the difference. At the end of the week I asked my colleagues if they had noticed anything different about me, and they all looked at me blankly and said no. I also discovered that I felt fine about myself in my dowdy old clothes. No matter what I had on, I still had a pretty good figure, was attractive and well groomed, and had a lot of self-confidence. What a surprise! I never would have thought I'd feel that comfortable if I didn't look smashing (in my eyes). If I hadn't gone average for that week, I never would have found that out.

13. If you shop for others (to buy their approval), experiment. Next time you go to see someone, do not bring a gift. Find out if the person still values you. You may discover that your friend not only likes you but is also relieved. Your constant gift giving may put pressure on others to reciprocate, even when they don't want to. Instead, give your friend a pat or a hug and tell them how much you enjoy them.

14. Don't anticipate or fantasy shop. Don't buy for a party you haven't been invited to or an interview that isn't set.

15. Throw out catalogs that come to your home. Go directly from the mailbox to the trash can. They're just too tempting to have around.

16. When you shop, take along a calculator. Add up your purchases as you go along, rather than just jamming the sales receipts into your purse. When it comes to overspending, vagueness is an accomplice.

17. If you think obsessively about shopping and just can't get it off your mind, don't try. Instead, each time you think about shopping, picture both shopping *and* something outlandish or eyecatching—like a red Volkswagen Beetle with polka dots or a giraffe. In time, both thoughts should disappear.

No one can guarantee happy endings all the time, but I honestly believe that if you follow the eleven-step program and take into account many of these suggestions you will be well on your way to having your shopping problem licked. It's important not to be hard on yourself; don't expect the problem to resolve itself all at once, but you will see *gradual* changes.

Vicki, who we've followed throughout the book, is a fine example of someone who has learned gradually, but also successfully, to cope with her shopping and related emotional problems.

Vicki: A Happier Ending

It had been at least six months since Vicki last came to therapy, so I called her up to see how she was doing. Her voice sounded strong and happy over the phone and her words confirmed that impression. She and Phil finally bought a home they both like. It isn't lavish, but that is not important to either of them. What matters to Vicki is that it's exactly what she wants—big enough for two people to live in comfortably, but the upkeep is not a hassle. For the first time in his married life, Phil parted with enough money for Vicki to buy all new furniture and decorate their new home, just as she has always wanted to. Also for the first time, Phil spoke up about the colors he likes, and so their home is decorated in a way that is pleasing to both of them.

Phil still slips now and then. He still talks down to his wife, but Vicki says she handles it in an entirely new way. When Phil is condescending or critical, they are able to discuss it calmly. More important, Vicki feels differently about such encounters inside because, she says, "I see options I never saw before. Before I'd go out and charge things to get even. But now when I'm bugged I can talk about it, ignore it, or laugh it off. When Phil and I do talk, things go differently. I now believe for the first time that he does the absolute best that he can, in his own way. He's changed a lot of little things." Phil's not putting so much pressure on Vicki to help out with the business, but she's volunteered to help out in projects that interest her. "I feel closer to him than I've ever felt. I get the same feeling back from him."

Phil and Vicki don't have sex, but that seems to be okay with both of them—although somehow I doubt that it's really agreeable to Phil. Phil has lost twenty pounds and is working on losing more. Perhaps he's hoping to look more attractive and woo Vicki back into bed. If that's the case, I'm afraid he's going to be sorely disappointed. Vicki simply doesn't like sex, and even though she and Phil are closer in other ways, her attitude about sex hasn't changed. Vicki, too, is just beginning to lose the weight she put on when she had to quit tennis for a while. This change appears to eliminate the all-too-frequent occurrence of addiction swapping. As mentioned earlier, shopping and overeating are the two most highly correlated quick fixes that women turn to when they're stressed. Now that Vicki's knee is healed, she's back on the courts again and says she never felt happier.

I like the ending of this story because it's realistic. Rarely are people able to change every single aspect of their lives to the point where everything is perfect. They're not with Vicki and Phil. Vicki is still not terribly assertive, but she's made enough changes to be aware that she has several options when she's feeling mistreated. She no longer has to shop to communicate.

Vicki's story underscores the note on which I'd like to conclude this book. Vicki was hurting when she entered therapy. She was ashamed about the money she'd spent, unclear about why she had done it, and acutely unhappy with certain parts of her marriage. Her spending was a symptom—a symptom that eventually got so out of hand that she could no longer ignore it. And in having to deal with her addiction, she was forced to confront the unhappiness in her life. Doing so wasn't nearly as painful as she feared. In a few short months, she found the strength and skills she needed to regain her self-respect and modify her marriage to the point where she is now reasonably content.

That seems to be the case with Jackie Onassis as well. Although she still binges now and then, she appears to have achieved happiness on a number of fronts. Not only is her work as an editor satisfying, but she is also genuinely happy with her mate, Maurice Tempelsman. Although the public may still be perplexed by her choice of mate, this choice may suggest something very healthy about her. She has always been a woman controlled and consumed by exteriors—the exterior of her own body, her clothes, her homes, and their furnishings. Perhaps her inner peace and higher self-esteem have allowed her to cast aside the superficial importance of youthful attractiveness and derive enormous pleasure from Maurice's intelligence and wit. With him, she seems content to relinquish the spotlight and quietly enjoy the pleasure of his company.

I have just gotten home from buying some new shoes. But they're not for me, they're for my horse Sweet William. The blacksmith came to the stable today, so William and I got to spend a couple of hours together while his four hooves were outfitted. At first we stood quietly together while Bill, the blacksmith, worked his way around William's warm, brown body. Then I sat on a rail facing William, and William put his soft nose to my chest so I could scratch his star-crested forehead and tickle him under his chin. The hours I spend with him are always like this. Peaceful and wondrous. Spiritual.

I'd love to tell you that I haven't been shopping in months or spent any money on indulgences, but that wouldn't be true. Last night, for instance, I bought this silk number for a bunch of satisfying events we have planned for the fall: the Kirov Ballet, season tickets to the opera, and a series of tickets to the symphony. But in rereading the personal goals I mentioned earlier in this chapter, I think I'm doing reasonably well. I have gone into debt a small amount to get some things now that I know I will need later, but I am also working harder and producing more income. I haven't been able to save a dime, but that, too, feels okay for the time being. What I have accomplished is to stop the slow erosion of our savings account; it's at about the same level as it was a year ago. That list of goals addressed the realities of money handling. It didn't talk to the quality of my life, which has become greatly enriched. Many of the activities I loved before are still a part of my life. But now there are all of the new joys I don't think I ever would have found if I hadn't become a shopaholic. That's the beauty of our symptoms. They're put in front of us so that we can experience a kind of psychic make-over. One that will leave us enriched and glowing as we trade in our charge cards for happier lives.

Bibliography

Baker, Jean H. *Mary Todd Lincoln*. New York: W. W. Norton, 1987.

Baran, Walter. "The TV Shopaholic." *Star,* January 19, 1988.

Birmingham, Stephen. *Jacqueline Bouvier Kennedy Onassis.* New York: Grosset and Dunlap, 1969.

Bodian, Stephan. "Addiction to Perfection, an Interview with Marion Woodman." *Yoga Journal,* November–December 1988.

Cassini, Oleg. "Dressing for Camelot." *People,* August 24, 1987.

"Catalogs." *San Jose Mercury News,* November 8, 1987.

Connell, Joan. "Harper's Editor Prophesies Doom for Narcissim." *San Jose Mercury News,* February 6, 1988.

Cronk, Michael. "Mall Walking Melds Health, Happiness, Security." *San Jose Mercury News,* April 15, 1987.

Darrach, Brad. "Prince Charles: A Dangerous Age." *People,* October 31, 1988.

Davids, John H. *The Kennedys, Dynasty and Disaster 1848–1983.* New York: McGraw-Hill, 1984.

Davidson, Joy. *The Agony of It All.* Los Angeles: Jeremy Tarcher, 1988.

Ellison, Katherine. *Steel Butterfly of the Philippines.* New York: McGraw-Hill, 1988.

Frondorf, Shirley. *Death of a "Jewish American Princess": The True Story of a Victim on Trial.* New York: Villard Books, 1988.

Gallagher, Mary Barelli. *My Life with Jacqueline Kennedy.* New York: David McCay, 1969.

Goldberg, Herbert, and Robert T. Lewis. *Money Madness*. New York: William Morrow, 1978.

Goldstein, Judith L. "Lifestyles of the Rich and Tyrannical. Spending habits of Imelda Marcos and Michele Duvalier." *American Scholar*. Spring 1987.

Graham, Ellen. "Kids Who Hold the Family Purse Strings." *Sunday Punch, San Francisco Chronicle*, January 31, 1988.

Green, Harvey, and Mary E. Perry, *The Light of the Home, An Intimate View of the Lives of Women In Victorian America*. New York: Pantheon, 1983.

Heymann, C. David. *A Woman Named Jackie*. New York: Lyle Stuart, 1989.

Heyn, Dalma. "The Big, Bad Buy." *Mademoiselle,* August 1987.

Holmes, Thomas H., and Richard H. Rache. "The Social Readjustment: Rating Scale." *Journal of Psychosomatic Research* 11 (1967).

"Imeldarabilia: A Final Count." *Time,* February 23, 1987.

Jampolsky, Gerald G. *Good-bye to Guilt*. Toronto: Bantam Books, 1985.

Kaufman, Steve. "Mall Wars." *San Jose Mercury News,* February 29, 1988.

Kavanaugh, Philip R. *Pathway to Recovery*. Los Gatos, Calif.: 1988.

Kelley, Kitty. *Jackie Oh!* New York: Ballantine Books, 1978.

Klein, Edward. "One Woman's Search for Love: A Profile of Audrey Hepburn." *Parade*. March 5, 1989.

Lapham, Lewis H. "Harper's Editor Prophesies Doom for Narcissism." San Jose Mercury News, Feb. 6, 1988.

Larsen, Earnie. *Stage II Recovery: Life Beyond Addiction*. San Francisco: Harper and Row, 1985.

Lerner, Harriet. *The Dance of Anger*. New York: Harper and Row, 1985.

Lindbergh, Anne Morrow. *Locked Rooms and Open Doors: Diaries and Letters 1933–1935*. New York: Harcourt Brace Jovanovich, 1974.

Martin, Ralph G. *Charles and Diana*. New York: Ivy Books, 1985.

Mercury News Wire Service. "Catalogs." *San Jose Mercury News*. November 8, 1987.

Morris, Betsey. "Big Spenders: As a Favored Pastime, Shopping Ranks High with Most Americans." *Wall Street Journal*, July 30, 1987.

Mundis, Jerrold. *How to Get Out of Debt, Stay Out of Debt and Live Prosperously*. New York: Bantam Books, 1988.

"The Oil Boom Went Bust, But the Mall Boom Blooms." *San Jose Mercury News*, April 21, 1988.

Pedrosa, Carmen Navarro. *Imelda Marcos*. New York: St. Martin's Press, 1987.

Randall, Ruth Painter. *Mary Lincoln: Biography of a Marriage*. Boston: Little, Brown, 1953.

Reid, Dixie. "Falling Victim to Charge Cards." *Tribune* (Oakland, Calif.).

Romulo, Beth Day. *Inside the Palace*. New York: G. P. Putnam and Sons, 1987.

Rosellini, Gayle, and Mark Worden. *Taming Your Turbulent Past*. Pompano Beach, Fla.: Health Communications, 1987.

Ross, Ishbel. *The President's Wife: Mary Todd Lincoln*. New York: G. P. Putnam and Sons, 1973.

Rothschild, Helen. *Free to Fly, Dare to Be a Success*. Saratoga, Calif.: R. and E. Press, 1986.

Schaef, Anne Wilson. *When Society Becomes an Addict*. San Francisco: Harper and Row, 1987.

Seward, Ingrid. *Diana: An Intimate Portrait*. Chicago: Contemporary Books, 1988.

Simmons, Dawn Langley. *A Rose for Mrs. Lincoln*. Boston: Beacon Press, 1970.

Smalley, Gary, and John Trent. *The Language of Love*. Pomona, Calif.: Focus on the Family Publishing, 1988.

Stephen, Barry P. *Royal Service: My Twelve Years as Valet to Prince Charles*. New York: Macmillan, 1983.

Storr, Anthony. *Churchill's Black Dog, Kafka's Mice and Other*

Phenomena of the Human Mind. New York: Grove Press, 1988.

Stuart, Mary S. *In Sickness and in Health: The Co-Dependent Marriage.* Deerfield Beach, Fla.: Health Communications, 1989.

Thomas, David, and Susie Pearson. "Diana: Her Secret Life." *Ladies' Home Journal,* February 1988.

von Oech, Roger. *A Whack on the Side of the Head.* New York: Warner Books, 1983.

Weiss, Mike. "Buy Me! Buy Me! Buy Me!" *West Magazine, San Jose Mercury News,* May 8, 1988.

White, Diane. "Sex or Shopping: Surprise Is in Store." *San Jose Mercury News,* November 18, 1987.

Witkin, Georgia. *Quick Fixes and Small Comforts.* New York: Villard Books, 1988.

Woititz, Janet G. *Struggle for Intimacy.* Pompano Beach, Fla.: Health Communications, 1985.

"Worst Stress News for Men." *Parade,* January 1, 1989.